# how2become

## Civil Service
## Fast Stream Test Guide

**www.How2Become.com**

As part of this product you have also received FREE access to online tests that will help you to pass the Civil Service Tests.

To gain access, simply go to:

**www.PsychometricTestsOnline.co.uk**

Get more products for passing any test or interview at:

**www.how2become.com**

Orders: Please contact How2become Ltd, Suite 2, 50 Churchill Square Business Centre, Kings Hill, Kent ME19 4YU.

You can order through Amazon.co.uk under ISBN 9781910602027, via the website www.How2Become.com or through Gardners.com.

ISBN: 9781910602027

First published in 2014 by How2become Ltd.

Typeset for How2become Ltd by Anton Pshinka.

## Disclaimer

Every effort has been made to ensure that the information contained within this guide is accurate at the time of publication. How2become Ltd are not responsible for anyone failing any part of any selection process as a result of the information contained within this guide. How2become Ltd and their authors cannot accept any responsibility for any errors or omissions within this guide, however caused. No responsibility for loss or damage occasioned by any person acting, or refraining from action, as a result of the material in this publication can be accepted by How2become Ltd.

The information within this guide does not represent the views of any third party service or organisation.

# CONTENTS

# CHAPTER 1

# *INTRODUCTION TO CIVIL SERVICE*

# WHAT IS THE CIVIL SERVICE?

The UK Civil Service plays a significant role as part of the Government. The Civil Service helps to develop and implement new policies and procedures and enforce them in society. Foremost, they not only work alongside the Government, but they are also the voices of society. They primarily provide a service directed to all people across the country in order to support and assist issues such as:

- Paying benefits
- Healthcare
- Providing pension schemes
- Operating effective prison systems
- Issuing driving licenses and a range of other important development policies.

People who work for the Civil Service are 'officials' who work under Government surveillance. They are co-ordinated and monitored by the Prime Minister to guarantee that policies are met and procedures are enforced. The Civil Service does not include all public sector employees. Employees of the police service, armed forces and local Government and Counsels, are not part of the Civil Service.

The Civil Service are impartial and objective people in terms of political movements. The service that they provide does not reflect a certain political party. It merely demonstrates a non-political stance that is used to effectively maintain and enhance community procedures and policies. In other words, even if the leading Government and political party changes; this has no effect on the Civil Service. The Civil Service remains unaffected and serves the Government in power.

The Civil Service comes with great responsibility. Her Majesty's Civil Service was imposed to instigate and execute important decisions made by the Government, and thus it plays a vital role in all segments of society including safety, security and stability.

The Civil Service play an accountable role in regards to both public and Government sectors. The Civil Service uses four key values to assess candidates:

- **Integrity** = the ability to put obligations of the public service above personal interests and/or beliefs.
- **Honesty** = being able to demonstrate high levels of truthfulness and openness.
- **Objectivity** = being able to display objective views and opinions on certain areas. Basing decisions and policies on rigorous analysis and evidence to form a plausible and valid outcome.
- **Impartiality** = being able to serve the power of the Government in charge and meet the needs and merits in which they enforce.

In order to provide the best practices and services, the Civil Service is constantly changing and adapting in order to remain current and relevant to the zeitgeists of society.

The Civil Service is a contemporary and diverse workplace that is solely committed to promoting and ensuring equality and diversity. As stated on the UK Government website, the Civil Service do not "unlawfully discriminate in any aspect of employment, including:

- How employees are selected
- Employment terms offered
- Whether employees are promoted or receive training, transfers or benefits
- How employees are trained.

The Civil Service's main priority is to instigate quality and diversity through public domains in order to serve a purpose for everyone in society. They need to ensure that policies and services that they provide reflect experiences of social, cultural and economical changes within society.

As a civil servant of the fast stream route you can expect to earn a starting salary between £25,000 and £27,000 per annum. Although this may not seem like a great deal, you can expect your pay to rise as your profession and experience level increases.

Like many jobs if you put in the effort, you will receive the benefits. Pay will undoubtedly increase if your performance excels. After 4-5 years, you could be earning over £45,000 if you are promoted and progress through the levels in the civil service.

# THE AIMS OF THE BOOK

This book is a learning aid for anyone wishing to pursue a career in the Civil Service. Understanding the different stages of the selection process is important. This book contains hundreds of practice questions that are very similar to the actual questions used in the Civil Service Fast Stream Tests. Therefore it is imperative you take the time to learn the question types and be fully prepared to successfully complete the test.

This learning aid is designed for people who wants to become part of the Civil Service via the Fast Stream route. If you are about to take, or thinking about taking the route of a Fast Stream applicant, you need to understand the processes and stages of the application.

The aim of this book is simple. It gives clear and detailed information on everything you will need to know in terms of the selection process and the Fast Stream tests.

# AIMS AND OBJECTIVES OF THE BOOK

The aims and objectives of this book are to provide:

- Confidence that you are 100% ready for the Civil Service Fast Stream Tests
- Detailed explanations given about each section of the tests so you know what to expect
- General tips for passing the application and selection process
- Lots and lots of questions for you to work through at your own pace
- Simple layouts which are easy to follow

# HOW TO WORK THROUGH THE BOOK

The book follows a simple structure. It solely focuses on the Fast Steam route into the Civil Service and thus provides all the information and practice questions you will need to know.

The book is broken down into sections displaying the types of tests you will face in the Fast Stream Tests. These include verbal reasoning, numerical reasoning and e-tray exercises. Each of these will be a significant part of the selection process and so you need to be able to pass each of these tests, in order to move on to the next stage.

Following each of these chapters will be a 'General Tips' chapter for you to understand how to pass each stage and ensure you are equipped with all the important information.

At the end of each sub-chapter, you will be able to check your answers. Make sure you do check your answers because it is just as important to know where you went wrong, as it is getting the question right. Take the time to thoroughly understand each question type to ensure maximum potential in progressing through the testing process.

We have deliberately provided you with lots of sample questions for you to practice to ensure that you are ready when it comes to taking the real test.

# STRUCTURE OF THE BOOK

The structure of the book will allow you to slowly and carefully identify each stage of the selection and application process. In order for you to be successful at passing the selection process, it is important that you have knowledge and clarity in regards to what is expected and how you should tackle each stage. Each stage needs to be passed in order for you to move on to the next stage of the application process.

This book will provide you with all the key information, practice and tips you will need to face your Civil Service Fast Stream Tests. This book includes:

- An Introduction to Fast Stream
- General tips for passing the Fast Stream
- Numerical Reasoning Tests
- Verbal Reasoning Tests
- E-Tray Exercises
- General tips for passing the E-Tray Exercises
- Assessment Centre
- General tips for passing the Assessment Centre
- Final Selection Board

Finally, we have also provided you with some additional free online psychometric tests which will help to further improve your competence in this particular testing area. To gain access, simply go to:

**www.PsychometricTestsOnline.co.uk**

Good luck and best wishes,

*The how2become team*

The How2become team

# CHAPTER 2

# *INTRODUCTION TO FAST STREAM*

The Civil Service Fast Stream Tests are designed as a talent and skill management programme for graduates with the potential of becoming leaders in the Civil Service. Applicants need to have at least a 2:2 degree in any subject to apply for a scheme in the Civil Service. The Fast Stream route offers graduates the opportunity to potentially make an impact on people's lives in both the United Kingdom and the rest of the world.

The Fast Stream is very competitive and highly advanced. Therefore it is important that you are fully prepared for every stage of the selection process.

This book will not only provide you with plenty of sample questions for you to test yourself, but it will also provide you with detailed and valuable insight into the selection process, what to expect, how to apply and general tips.

The Civil Service Fast Steam is open to applicants who are:

- University graduates with at least a 2:2 in any degree subject
- British citizens
- European Economic Area (EEA) nationals
- Commonwealth citizens
- Swiss nationals
- And in some circumstance, Turkish nationals.

The difference between the Fast Stream and other routes into the Civil Service is the 'speed'. As an applicant of the Fast Stream route, you will be able to progress more quickly through the grades of the Civil Service. Therefore, you will be expected to provide higher levels of experience, knowledge and skills that are required for any of the Fast Stream schemes.

## TYPES OF ROLES

There are many Fast Stream options which you can choose from when applying for a Fast Stream job in the Civil Service.

Below is a list of the types of roles you can apply for. Each job role has a brief description along with the qualification requirements needed.

## GENERALIST OPTIONS

| FAST STREAM OPTIONS | WHAT YOU NEED TO GET IN | TYPES OF ROLE |
|---|---|---|
| Central Departments | 2:2 in any degree subject | Operational Delivery, Policy Development, Financial Management, People Management, Corporate Services |
| Diplomatic Service | 2:2 in any degree subject<br><br>Must be British citizen (dual nationality may apply)<br><br>Must have been a UK resident for 2 out of the last 10 years | Operational Delivery, Policy Development, Corporate Services, Overseas Posting |
| Houses of Parliament | 2:2 in any degree subject | Clerks |
| Science and Engineering | Doctorate or Master's degree in biological, physical, computational or<br><br>mathematical science or engineering subject<br><br>or<br><br>chartered engineer registered by one of the 36 professional engineering<br><br>institutions licensed by the Engineering Council<br><br>or<br><br>1st or 2:1 in<br><br>undergraduate degree with at least one mathematical module | Defence, Security, Climate, Health, Energy, Animal Welfare |

## ANALYTICAL OPTIONS

| FAST STREAM OPTIONS | WHAT YOU NEED TO GET IN | TYPES OF ROLE |
|---|---|---|
| Economist | 2:1 or postgraduate degree in economics<br><br>Joint degree accepted if 50% of modules are in economics | Government Economics |
| Statistician | 2:1 degree in a numerate discipline e.g. Maths, Economics, Psychology or Geography | Statistics |
| Operational Researcher | 2:1 numerate degree or 2:2 with a relevant postgraduate qualification | Analyst |
| Social Researcher | 2:1 degree in social science or 2:2 with a relevant postgraduate qualification in social research | Research Officer |

## COMMERCIAL OPTIONS

| FAST STREAM OPTIONS | WHAT YOU NEED TO GET IN | TYPES OF ROLE |
|---|---|---|
| Finance | 2:1 in any degree subject | Finance Specialist |
| Internal Audit | 2:1 in any degree subject | Auditor |
| Commercial | 2:1 in any degree subject | Procurement Category Management, Commercial Management, Customer Service/Delivery, Policy |

## GOVERNMENT OPTIONS

| FAST STREAM OPTIONS | WHAT YOU NEED TO GET IN | TYPES OF ROLE |
|---|---|---|
| Communications | 2:1 in any degree subject | Media and Press Management, Marketing, Digital Communications |

## HUMAN RESOURCES OPTIONS

| FAST STREAM OPTIONS | WHAT YOU NEED TO GET IN | TYPES OF ROLE |
|---|---|---|
| Human Resources | 2:2 in any degree subject | HR Operations and Policy |

## EUROPEAN OPTIONS

| FAST STREAM OPTIONS | WHAT YOU NEED TO GET IN | TYPES OF ROLE |
|---|---|---|
| Europe | 2:2 in any degree subject<br><br>A to C grade at A-Level French or German | EU Policy, Corporate and Operational Policies |

## DIGITAL AND TECHNOLOGY

| FAST STREAM OPTIONS | WHAT YOU NEED TO GET IN | TYPES OF ROLE |
|---|---|---|
| Digital and Technology | 2:1 in any degree | Product Design, Content Analysis, Corporate Services, Software Engineering, Operations, Strategy and Policy |

The Fast Stream process requires applicants who possess strong levels of verbal and numerical ability. Fast Stream tests are designed to measure your writing skills, analytical skills, interpersonal skills, decision making abilities and numerical reasoning.

These tests are primarily meant to determine strong candidates who show the abilities needed to become a civil servant. It is important that you fully comprehend what the tests involve, the types of questions you might be faced with and how to reach the correct answer.

# STAGES OF APPLICATION PROCESS

ONLINE **SELF ASSESSMENT** TESTS **1**

ONLINE **PRACTICE** TESTS **2**

ONLINE **SELECTION** TESTS **3**

ONLINE **SELECTION AND APPLIACTION** FORM **4**

ANALYTICAL **SPECIALIST** ASSESSMENT **5**
Economist, Operational Researcher, Social Researcher, Statistician etc

ONLINE **E-TRAY** TESTS **6**

ONE DAY **FAST STREAM ASSESSMENT** CENTRE **7**

FINAL **SELECTION** BOARD **8**

Once you have decided to apply for the Fast Stream route, you have a limited time to complete your application. In other words, once you pick your selected scheme or schemes that you want to apply for, you have a number of steps to follow which need to be performed in the allocated timescale.

- **Self-Assessment Reasoning Tests** – these tests are only to be taken if you are applying for the Generalist or Northern Ireland Fast Stream route. These tests consist of two parts =

    - **Verbal reasoning** – 40 questions, 20 minutes
    - **Numerical reasoning** – 18 questions, 22 minutes (dealing with percentages, fractions, ratios, multiplication, averages, decimals).

- **Practice Online Tests** – This is not a necessary requirement but it is considered highly beneficial for anyone who wants to be successful at passing the Civil Service Tests. They are a good way to judge how well you might do when it comes to the real test. These tests consist of verbal and numerical reasoning.

- **Situational Judgement** – this test will provide you with a variety of scenarios by which you need to answer the following questions. You will be given 15 different scenarios, each of which will contain 4 potential responses/outcomes. Your task is simply to judge the situation based on the information you have been provided with. This test is not timed.

- **Online Selection Tests** – this is an extremely crucial stage of the selection process. Your results from this test will determine whether or not you will proceed to the next stage of the application process. This is why if you are serious about successfully passing these tests, you should heavily practice the online tests, as previously mentioned. The test will comprise of:

    - **Verbal reasoning** – 40 questions, 20 minutes
    - **Numerical reasoning** – 20 questions, 25 minutes
    - **Fast stream competency** – multiple choice (not timed but allow 35 minutes for completion).

- **Analytical Fast Stream Assessment** – depending on what area of the Civil Service you are applying for, you may be asked to attend a half-day assessment in London whereby your technical and analytical skills will be put to the test.

- **E-Tray Exercise** – this exercise will test your ability to handle lots of data and information. The test is typical of the requests that you may be faced with in the life of a Fast Streamer. The test takes approximately two hours. The E-Tray exercise is broken down into three sections:

  1. Reading and comprehending background information.
  2. Identifying the most and least effective responses to a number of emails.
  3. Writing responses to requests, using the information you have already been provided.

- **Final Assessment** – after completing your e-tray test, candidates are shortlisted and invited to a one-day assessment at the Fast Stream Assessment Centre in London (FSAC). The day will comprise of a written assessment, leadership and group exercises, and an interview.

- **Final Selection Board** – depending on the scheme you have applied for, will determine whether or not you need to attend the Final Selection Board. This is similar to the Assessment Centre in that your skills, knowledge and competencies will be put to the test. Please note, only certain schemes/ options require you to partake in this stage, it may not apply to you. The final selection process at the Final Selection Board is only relevant if you are applying for one of these options:

  - Diplomatic services
  - European
  - Houses of parliament
  - Digital and technology
  - Science and engineering
  - Government communication services

# CHAPTER 3

# *GENERAL TIPS FOR PASSING FAST STREAM*

# GENERAL TIPS FOR PASSING THE FAST STREAM TESTS

- Practice makes perfect! Ensure that you are fully prepared by familiarising yourself with the test.

- Be prepared! It is important that you are prepared for your tests which is why practicing plenty of sample questions is the best solution.

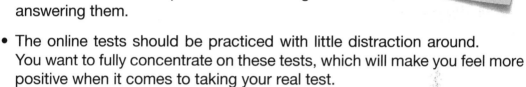

- Read everything carefully and ensure you understand what the questions are asking before answering them.

- The online tests should be practiced with little distraction around. You want to fully concentrate on these tests, which will make you feel more positive when it comes to taking your real test.

- Remember, these tests are here to analyse your abilities and knowledge and assess whether you are a valuable candidate for the Civil Service.

- Stay calm, stay focused and stay positive!

- Make sure you are familiar with using a calculator. For the Fast Stream tests this will be your lifeline. If you do not know how to work it, you are going to struggle.

- Ensure your mathematical skills are up to scratch. Try practicing numerical, psychometric, data interpretation and quantitative reasoning tests to ensure your numerical skills are bettered.

- The tests involve working with fine lines distinguishing between the right and wrong answer. Therefore, you need to fully comprehend all of the information you are presented with and ensure you know what is being asked.

- The first part of your application consists of a self-assessment. Be sure to present yourself in the best possible way. If your application has silly errors in terms of grammar and punctuation, chances are your application will get rejected. It is imperative to make a good impression.

- Your application needs to be registered online where you will receive a password to access your email. Regularly check your inbox to make sure you receive all the information and notifications.

- Practice, practice, practice! Ensure yourself with the best possible start in your application process by undertaking lots of practice questions and gain full understanding of what is expected. The more you practice, the more likely you will succeed and the better prepared you will feel in the exam.

- Timing is key. The 'fast' in Fast Stream means that you will be assessed under strict time limits, which most candidates find limiting, so you need to work on your timing skills.

# CHAPTER 4

# NUMERICAL
# REASONING TESTS

## (SUBSECTION 1)

Fast Streamers will need to take the Numerical Reasoning Test. Candidates will be provided with numerical data, usually in the form of graphs, charts, statistics or financial data. For these questions, you should carefully analyse the data provided and then answer the following questions in relation to that data.

For the real test, you can expect to answer approximately 20 questions in a time frame of 25 minutes. However, this chapter will provide you with lots of practice questions for you to work through. We have deliberately chosen to do this so you are fully prepared and gain a wider understanding of how to answer these questions.

Before you begin this testing section, let's take a look at the below example:

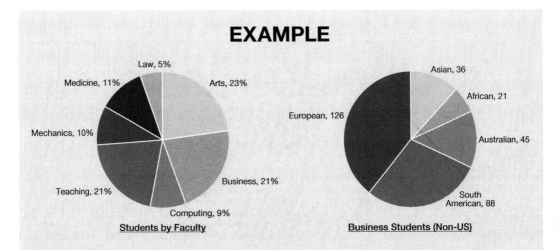

## Question

If there are a total of 1098 students in the Business faculty, how many students are there in total at the university?

## How to work it out

You know 1098 students = business faculty. The business faculty accounts for 21% of the whole of the university.

- 1098 x 100 / 21(%) = 5228

## Answer

5228

You will experience these types of data interpretation questions on your fast stream tests. The following pages contain 100 numerical practice questions, each with an explanation to obtain the answer. The answers and explanations can be found at the end of every sub-section.

We have deliberately not provided you with a time limit. This will allow you to work through these questions carefully and at a pace that suits you.

Please circle the correct answer.

The following table shows the percentage of copper in two coins

| COIN | WEIGHT | COPPER |
|------|--------|--------|
| 50p coin | 8g | 25% |
| 20p coin | 5g | 16% |

## Question 1

If both the coins are made of only nickel and copper, what is the difference between the weight of nickel present in the 50 pence coin and the weight of nickel in the 20 pence coin?

| A | B | C | D | E |
|---|---|---|---|---|
| 1.2g | 0.8g | 1.8g | 1.25g | 0.75g |

## Question 2

What is the difference in percentages from the amount of copper in the 50p coin compared to the copper in the 20p coin?

| A | B | C | D | E |
|---|---|---|---|---|
| 11% | 4% | 3% | 9% | 5% |

## Question 3

What would be the weight (grams) of nickel if you had eight 50p coins?

| A | B | C | D | E |
|---|---|---|---|---|
| 12g | 32g | 40g | 11g | 48g |

## Question 4

What is the difference between the amount of nickel in the 50p coin and the nickel in the 20p coin? Write your answer as a decimal. Write your answer as a decimal in grams.

| A | B | C | D | E |
|---|---|---|---|---|
| 1.8g | 1.4g | 2.8g | 2.25g | 1g |

Mineral water is classified on the basis of the amount of dissolved solid materials it contains. The chart shows the codes of different levels of total dissolved solids (TDS) and the number of mineral water bottles for each code sold at a store.

| MINERAL WATER BOTTLES | | |
|---|---|---|
| Code | TDS  (mg/l) | Number of bottles |
| TDS 1 | Less than 50 | 52 |
| TDS 2 | Greater than or equal to 50 but less than 500 | 85 |
| TDS 3 | Greater than or equal to 500 but less than 1,500 | 65 |
| TDS 4 | Greater than or equal to 1,500 | 50 |

## Question 5

What fraction of the total number of bottles sold at the store with TDS greater than or equal to 50 mg/l, have the code TDS 4?

| A | B | C | D | E |
|---|---|---|---|---|
| 1/5 | 1/6 | 1/2 | 1/4 | 3/5 |

## Question 6

What fraction of the total number of bottles sold at the store with TDS greater than or equal to 500 mg/l, have the code TDS 3?

| A | B | C | D | E |
|---|---|---|---|---|
| 11/21 | 13/23 | 15/17 | 3/4 | 4/5 |

## Question 7

What is the difference of the number of bottles with TDS less than 50 and the number of bottles with TDS equal to or greater than 500?

| A | B | C | D | E |
|---|---|---|---|---|
| 41 | 32 | 87 | 63 | 53 |

## Question 8

How many bottles have TDS greater than or equal to 50?

| A | B | C | D | E |
|---|---|---|---|---|
| 115 | 85 | 65 | 50 | 200 |

| Company | Company Profit (Annual) (£) | Cost to buy company (£) | Number of employees |
|---------|------------------------------|-------------------------|---------------------|
| A | 15,000 | 18,000 | 6 |
| B | 26,000 | 24,000 | 11 |
| C | 22,000 | 20,000 | 8 |
| D | 40,000 | 40,000 | 10 |

## Question 9

Which company has the lowest annual profit per employee?

| A | B | C | D | E |
|---|---|---|---|---|
| Company A | Company B | Company C | Company D | Company C and D |

## Question 10

Approximately how many more employees would company C have to employ to achieve annual profit of £44,000?

| A | B | C | D | E |
|---|---|---|---|---|
| 4 | 11 | 8 | 3 | 19 |

## Question 11

If company A makes an annual profit of £31,000 the following year, what is the percentage increase?

| A | B | C | D | E |
|---|---|---|---|---|
| 106.6% | 94.5% | 6.6% | 51.6% | 103.2% |

## Question 12

If company D makes an annual profit of £15,000 the following year, what is the percentage decrease?

| A | B | C | D | E |
|---|---|---|---|---|
| 105.6% | 62.5% | 33.5% | 101.25% | 71% |

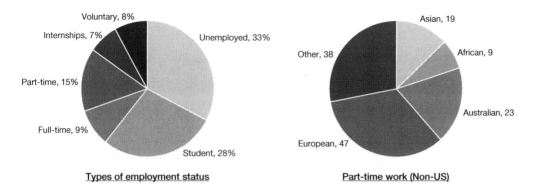

Types of employment status          Part-time work (Non-US)

The pie chart above shows the percentage of teenagers in different employment statuses and the number of non-US part time workers. These percentages have been rounded to the nearest whole number. There are a total of 982 teenagers in part time work. Use this information to answer the following questions.

## Question 13

How many teenagers are there altogether? Round to the nearest whole person.

| A | B | C | D | E |
|---|---|---|---|---|
| 6654 | 6546 | 5465 | 4456 | 4654 |

## Question 14

What percentage of teenagers in part time work are non-US teenagers? To the nearest whole number.

| A | B | C | D | E |
|---|---|---|---|---|
| 14% | 18% | 20% | 22% | 24% |

## Question 15

There are 64 European Interns. What percentage of the employment status does this represent? Round to the nearest whole number.

| A | B | C | D | E |
|---|---|---|---|---|
| 11% | 14% | 15% | 16% | 19% |

## Question 16

If 48 percent of students are European, how many European students are there?

| A | B | C | D | E |
|---|---|---|---|---|
| 822 | 813 | 867 | 897 | 879 |

Candidates Enrolled = 4800

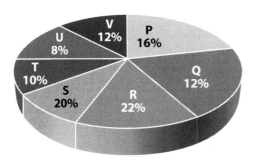

Candidates who passed the selection process = 1600

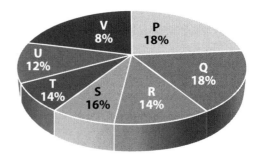

## Question 17

What is the ratio of candidates who passed the selection process to the candidates that enrolled from institute V?

| A | B | C | D | E |
|---|---|---|---|---|
| 1:3 | 2:9 | 11:13 | 4:5 | 3:7 |

## Question 18

What is the percentage of candidates passed to the candidates enrolled for institutes P and Q together? Round it to the nearest whole number.

| A | B | C | D | E |
|---|---|---|---|---|
| 11% | 56% | 43% | 49% | 9% |

## Question 19

The number of candidates passed from institutes R and S together is less than the number of candidates that enrolled from institutes U and T by:

| A | B | C | D | E |
|---|---|---|---|---|
| 384 | 264 | 184 | 394 | 96 |

## Question 20

What percentage of candidates passed the selection process from institute U out of the total number of candidates enrolled from the same institute? Round it to the nearest whole number.

| A | B | C | D | E |
|---|---|---|---|---|
| 65% | 75% | 25% | 50% | 15% |

# ANSWERS TO NUMERICAL REASONING – SUBSECTION 1

**Q1.** C

EXPLANATION = 8 / 100 x 75 = 6g,   5 / 100 x 84 = 4.2g,   6 – 4.2 = 1.8g.

**Q2.** D

EXPLANATION = 25 – 16 = 9%.

**Q3.** E

EXPLANATION = 8 / 100 x 75 = 6. 6 x 8 = 48g.

**Q4.** A

EXPLANATION = 8 / 100 x 75 = 6   5 / 100 x 84 = 4.2   So, 6 – 4.2 = 1.8g

**Q5.** D

EXPLANATION = 85 + 65 + 50 = 200. No. of bottles with TDS 4 = 50.   50/200 = 1/4.

**Q6.** B

EXPLANATION = 65 + 50 = 115,   No. of bottles with TDS 3 = 65,   65/115 = 13/23.

**Q7.** D

EXPLANATION = No. of bottles less than 50 = 52. No. of bottles more than 500 = 115,   115 – 52 = 63.

**Q8.** E

EXPLANATION = 85 + 65 + 50 = 200.

**Q9.** B

EXPLANATION = simply divide the annual profit for each company by the number of employees, and see which company has the lowest profits.

**Q10.** C

EXPLANATION = 44,000 / 2750 = 16. That is 8 more than what they have already.

**Q11.** A

EXPLANATION = 31,000 – 15,000 = 16,000,   16,000 / 15,000 x 100 = 106.6%.

**Q12.** B

EXPLANATION = 40,000 − 15,000 = 25,000,   25,000 / 40,000 x 100 = 62.5%.

**Q13.** B

EXPLANATION = Total no. of teenagers in part time work (982). So, 982 x 100 / 15 (percentage of part time status) = 6546.

**Q14.** A

EXPLANATION = 136 / 982 (no. of part time teenagers) x 100 = 13.97%. Nearest whole number = 14%.

**Q15.** B

EXPLANATION = 64 / 458 (no. of interns, 7% of 6546) x 100 = 13.97%. Nearest whole number = 14%.

**Q16.** E

EXPLANATION = 6546 / 100 x 28 = 1832. So, 1832 / 100 x 48 = 879.

**Q17.** B

EXPLANATION = 8 x 1600 / 12 x 4800 = 12800:57600 = 2:9.

**Q18.** C

EXPLANATION = 36 x 1600 = 57600. 28 x 4800 = 134400. So, 57600 / 134400 x 100 = 42.85%.

**Q19.** A

EXPLANATION = 30% of 1600, 18% of 4800,   864 − 480 = 384.

**Q20.** D

EXPLANATION = 12 x 1600 / 8 x 4800 x 100 = 50%.

# NUMERICAL REASONING TESTS

## (SUBSECTION 2)

### ANNUAL PERCENT CHANGE IN DOLLAR AMOUNT OF SALES AT FIVE RETAIL STORES FROM 2005 TO 2007

| STORE | PERCENT CHANGE FROM 2005 TO 2006 | PERCENT CHANGE FROM 2006 TO 2007 |
|-------|----------------------------------|----------------------------------|
| P | -20 | 8 |
| Q | -10 | 10 |
| R | 6 | 10 |
| S | -9 | -14 |
| T | 16 | -6 |

## Question 1

If the dollar amount of sales at store Q was $600,000 for 2005, what was the dollar amount of sales at the store in 2007?

| A | B | C | D | E |
|---|---|---|---|---|
| $625,000 | $594,000 | $660,000 | $315,000 | $543,000 |

## Question 2

At store T, the dollar amount of sales for 2006 was what percent of the dollar amount of sales for 2007? Give your answer to the nearest 0.1 percent.

| A | B | C | D | E |
|---|---|---|---|---|
| 36.4% | 102.3% | 106.4% | 110.4% | 64.6% |

## Question 3

The dollar amount of sales at store S for 2007 was more than 21 percent less than that for 2005. True or False?

| A | B |
|---|---|
| True | False |

## Question 4

The dollar amount of sales at store R for 2007 was more than 16 percent greater than that for 2005.

| A | B |
|---|---|
| True | False |

# Family tree

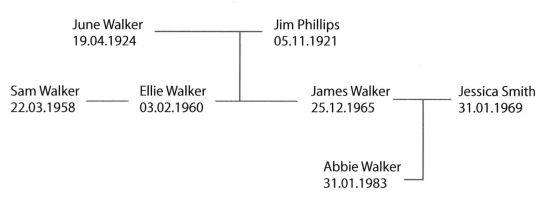

## Question 5

How old will Abbie be on 31.01.1999?

| A | B | C | D | E |
|---|---|---|---|---|
| 13 | 14 | 15 | 16 | 17 |

## Question 6

Sam dies before Abbie is born. James was 16 when Sam died. How old was Sam when he died?

| A | B | C | D | E |
|---|---|---|---|---|
| 17 | 23 | 19 | 25 | 28 |

## Question 7

How much older is Jessica compared to Abbie?

| A | B | C | D | E |
|---|---|---|---|---|
| 10 years | 11 years | 12 years | 13 years | 14 years |

## Question 8

June passed away on the 07.08.1994. How old was she?

| A | B | C | D | E |
|---|---|---|---|---|
| 70 | 74 | 65 | 82 | 86 |

### NSR500 Motorcycle sales

| Country | Jan | Feb | Mar | April | May | June | Total |
|---|---|---|---|---|---|---|---|
| UK | 32 | 36 | 28 | 21 | 42 | 46 | 205 |
| Germany | 42 | 51 | 53 | 49 | 41 | 35 | 271 |
| France | 12 | 18 | 21 | 15 | 28 | 21 | 115 |
| Belgium | 16 | 18 | 19 | 22 | 21 | 25 | 121 |
| Spain | 35 | 31 | 26 | 27 | 31 | 35 | 185 |
| Italy | 35 | 38 | 41 | 28 | 36 | 42 | 220 |
| Total | 172 | 192 | 188 | 162 | 199 | 204 | 1117 |

The above table shows the sales across 6 European countries for the NSR500 Motorcycle for a 6 month period. The NSR500 Motorcycle is imported to each country from a main dealer. Use the information provided to answer the following questions. Please circle the correct answer.

## Question 9

What percentage of total imports is accounted for by the three smallest importers?

| A | B | C | D | E |
|---|---|---|---|---|
| 27.8% | 31.7% | 37.7% | 42.7% | 37.1% |

## Question 10

What is the difference between the average number of units per month imported by Spain over the first 4 months and the average number of units per month imported by the UK over the first 4 months?

| A | B | C | D | E |
|---|---|---|---|---|
| 0.5 | 1.5 | 2 | 4 | 5.5 |

## Question 11

What percentage of the overall total sales were sold to Italian importers?

| A | B | C | D | E |
|---|---|---|---|---|
| 18.7% | 21.7% | 28.4% | 21.3% | 19.7% |

## Question 12

What month saw the biggest increase in total sales from the previous month?

| A | B | C | D | E |
|---|---|---|---|---|
| January | February | March | April | May |

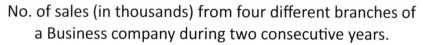

No. of sales (in thousands) from four different branches of a Business company during two consecutive years.

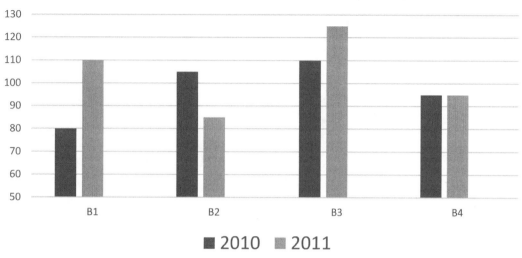

■ 2010  ■ 2011

## Question 13

Total sales of branches 1, 3 and 4 for both years (in thousands) is?

| A | B | C | D | E |
|---|---|---|---|---|
| 490 | 585 | 615 | 605 | 710 |

## Question 14

What was the percentage increase for Branch 1 from 2010 to 2011?

| A | B | C | D | E |
|---|---|---|---|---|
| 55% | 42.5% | 33.5% | 37.5% | 46.5% |

## Question 15

What was the percentage decrease for Branch 2 from 2010 to 2011?

| A | B | C | D | E |
|---|---|---|---|---|
| 19.05% | -19.1% | 22.4% | 13.05% | 17% |

## Question 16

Total sales of branch 4 for both years is what percent of the total sales of branch 3 for both years?

| A | B | C | D | E |
|---|---|---|---|---|
| 20.15% | 65.25% | 35.65% | 80.85% | 70.5% |

Ratio of exports and imports for two manufacturing companies

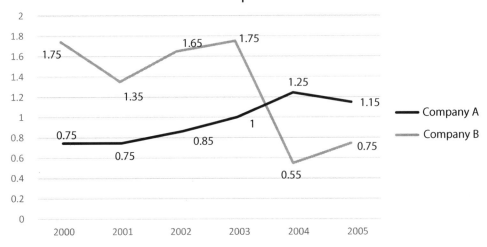

## Question 17

What is the difference between the number of imports and exports for company A in 2000 compared to the number of imports and exports for company B in 2005?

| A | B | C | D | E |
|---|---|---|---|---|
| 0 | 0.1 | 0.25 | 0.75 | 3 |

## Question 18

In how many of the years were the exports more than the imports for Company B?

| A | B | C | D | E |
|---|---|---|---|---|
| 1 | 2 | 3 | 4 | 5 |

## Question 19

In what year was the difference between the imports to exports the maximum for Company B?

| A | B | C | D | E |
|---|---|---|---|---|
| 2000 | 2001 | 2002 | 2003 | Cannot be determined |

## Question 20

If the exports for Company A in 2002 were 250, what was the amount of imports in that year?

| A | B | C | D | E |
|---|---|---|---|---|
| 220 | 196 | 294 | 274 | 312 |

# ANSWERS TO NUMERICAL REASONING – SUBSECTION 2

### Q1. B

EXPLANATION = $600,000 – 10% = $540,000. $540,000 + 10% of $540,000 = $594,000.

### Q2. C

EXPLANATION = If A is the dollar amount of sales at store T, from 2006 to 2007 there was a decrease by -6. 6 divided by 100 = 0.06, which means 0.94 is the dollar amount for 2007. Therefore, you need to divide A by 0.94. So 1 divided by 0.94 = 1.06382... To work out the percentage, multiply this by 100 to give you 106.38. To 1 decimal place and thus, the correct answer is 106.4%.

### Q3. A

EXPLANATION = if B is the dollar amount of sales at store S for 2005, then the dollar amount for 2006 is 0.91 % of B: (100 – 9 = 91. 91/100 = 0.91). The dollar amount for 2007 would be (100 – 14 = 86. 86/100 = 0.86). So, 0.91 x 0.86 = 0.7826, as a percent = 78.26. So, this represents a percent decrease of 100 – 78.26 = 21.74%, which is more than 21% so the statement must be true.

### Q4. A

EXPLANATION = If C is the dollar amount of sales at store R for 2005, then the dollar amount for 2006 is given by 1.06 and the dollar amount for 2007 is given by 1.10. So, 1.10 x 1.06 = 1.166. Note this represents a 16.6% increase, which is greater than 16%, so the answer must be true.

### Q5. D

EXPLANATION = 1999 - 1983 = 16 years.

### Q6. B

EXPLANATION = James was 16 = 1965 + 16 = 1981. So Sam died in 1981, 1981 – 1958 = 23.

### Q7. E

EXPLANATION = 1983 – 1969 = 14.

### Q8. A

EXPLANATION = 1994 – 1924 = 70.

**Q9.** C

EXPLANATION = to work out the percentage overall for the imports accounted by the three smallest importers, divide the total (1117) by how many motorcycles were sold from the three smallest importers (France, Belgium and Spain = 115 + 121 + 185 = 421) and then multiply it by 100. So, (421 / 1117 x 100 = 37.690) Rounded up to 1 decimal place = 37.7.

**Q10.** A

EXPLANATION = to work out the difference between averages for UK and Spain in the first 4 months, add up first 4 months for the UK (32 + 36 + 28 + 21 = 117), then divide it by how many numbers there are (4). (117 / 4 = 29.25). For Spain (35 + 31 + 26 + 27 = 119), then divide it by 4 = 29.75. So, the difference between UK (29.25) and Spain (29.75) = 0.50.

**Q11.** E

EXPLANATION = to work out the percentage overall total that was sold to Italian importers, divide the total (1117) by how many NSR500's were sold to Italian importers (220) and then multiply it by 100. So, (220 / 1117 x 100 = 19.69) Rounded up to 1 decimal place = 19.7.

**Q12.** E

EXPLANATION = to work out the biggest increase in total sales from the previous month, you work out the difference between the totals for each of the months and work out which has the biggest increase. Between April and May, there was an increase by 37. None of the other months have a bigger increase and therefore May is the correct answer.

**Q13.** C

EXPLANATION = 80 + 110 + 110 + 125 + 95 + 95 = 615 (thousand).

**Q14.** D

EXPLANATION = 110,000 – 80,000 = 30,000   30,000 / 80,000 x 100 = 37.5%.

**Q15.** A

EXPLANATION = 105,000 – 85,000 = 20,000   20,000 / 105 x 100 = 19.047 = 19.05%.

**Q16.** D

EXPLANATION = 95 + 95 = 190, 110 + 125 = 235   190 / 235 x 100 = 80.85%.

**Q17.** A

EXPLANATION = the number of imports and exports for company A in 2000 = 0.75. The number of imports and exports for Company B in 2005 = 0.75. Difference = 0.

**Q18.** D

EXPLANATION = if the ratio export to import is greater than 1, it means that the export was more than the import. For company B, the years 2000, 2001, 2002 and 2003 all have more than 1.

**Q19.** E

EXPLANATION = it cannot be determined based on the information provided. You do not have any statistical data to work out the difference between exports and imports.

**Q20.** C

EXPLANATION = 250 (the amount you are working out) / 0.85 (exports in 2002 for Company A) = 294.

# NUMERICAL
# REASONING TESTS

## (SUBSECTION 3)

|  | UK POUND STERLING (£) | US DOLLARS ($) |
|---|---|---|
| 1.00 UK pound | £1.00 | $1.59 |
| 1.00 US dollar | £0.62 | $1.00 |
| 1.00 Canadian dollar | £0.55 | $0.87 |
| 1.00 Euro | £0.78 | $1.24 |
| 1.00 Russian Ruble | £0.01 | $0.02 |

## Question 1

What is the approximate value in Pounds Sterling of 150 Euros?

| A | B | C | D | E |
|---|---|---|---|---|
| £78.50 | £117 | £101 | £107 | £77 |

## Question 2

How many dollars is 70 Russian Rubles worth?

| A | B | C | D | E |
|---|---|---|---|---|
| $0.80 | $1.20 | $1.40 | $1.80 | Cannot say |

## Question 3

How many more Canadian dollars would you have got for 100 pounds sterling than you would for 140 US dollars?

| A | B | C | D | E |
|---|---|---|---|---|
| CAD$52 | CAD$200 | CAD$36 | CAD$21 | CAD$56 |

## Question 4

How many more US dollars would you have got for 150 pounds sterling than you would for 100 Euros?

| A | B | C | D | E |
|---|---|---|---|---|
| $105.50 | $112.75 | $85.75 | $95.70 | $114.50 |

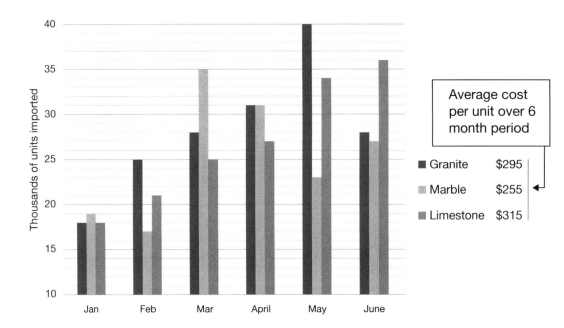

## Question 5
What was the difference in thousands of units between granite stone and marble stone imported in the first 5 months of the year?

| A | B | C | D | E |
|---|---|---|---|---|
| 11 | 13 | 15 | 17 | 19 |

## Question 6
Which month showed the largest total increase in the number of units (thousands) over the 6 month period?

| A | B | C | D | E |
|---|---|---|---|---|
| January | February | March | April | May |

## Question 7
What was the ratio of marble and limestone for the 6 month period?

| A | B | C | D | E |
|---|---|---|---|---|
| 152:161 | 90:105 | 31:37 | 5:7 | 9:11 |

## Question 8
What was the percentage of granite stone imported over the 6 month period?

| A | B | C | D | E |
|---|---|---|---|---|
| 40.5% | 42.2% | 35.2% | 38.7% | 39% |

| COMPANY | ACTUAL INCOME (ANNUAL) for 2001 | TARGET INCOME (ANNUAL) for 2001 |
|---|---|---|
| Company A | £234,570 | £300,000 |
| Company B | £420,000 | £421,560 |
| Company C | £215,750 | £450,000 |
| Company D | £310,250 | £325,000 |
| Company E | £375,995 | £325,000 |

## Question 9

What is the percentage increase from the target income and the actual income for Company E?

| A | B | C | D | E |
|---|---|---|---|---|
| 13.7% | 15.7% | 19.7% | 17.7% | 7% |

## Question 10

Which company was the furthest away from their targeted annual income?

| A | B | C | D | E |
|---|---|---|---|---|
| Company A | Company B | Company C | Company D | Company E |

## Question 11

In the following year, Company B earns £275,000. What is the percentage decrease from Company B's earnings in 2001 and the earnings in the following year?

| A | B | C | D | E |
|---|---|---|---|---|
| 65.5% | 45.5% | 39.5% | 34.5% | 41.5% |

## Question 12

In the following year, Company E earns 23% more than their total income in 2001. How much does Company E earn in the following year? To the nearest whole number.

| A | B | C | D | E |
|---|---|---|---|---|
| £462,474 | £864,315 | £516,775 | £418,225 | £436,747 |

| Occupation | Average Salary for 2011 | Percent change from 2011 - 2012 |
|---|---|---|
| Consultants | £54,470 | 7% |
| Accountancy (Qualified) | £48,974 | -11% |
| Financing | £46,572 | 23% |
| IT | £42,716 | 13% |
| Construction | £41,741 | -4% |
| Legal | £38,270 | 26% |
| Human Resources | £37,804 | -10% |
| Marketing | £36,690 | -18% |
| Sales | £35,528 | 8% |
| Engineering | £35,515 | -11% |

## Question 13

What was the average income for the following year for people working in IT?

| A | B | C | D | E |
|---|---|---|---|---|
| £43,889 | £84,269 | £48,962 | £48,629 | £48,269 |

## Question 14

What was the average income in 2012 for people working in Human Resources?

| A | B | C | D | E |
|---|---|---|---|---|
| £31,040 | £34,024 | £33,402 | £33,023 | £35,500 |

## Question 15

What is the difference between the average salaries for Consultants in 2012 compared with average salaries for Engineering in 2012? To the nearest whole number.

| A | B | C | D | E |
|---|---|---|---|---|
| £58,282 | £31,606 | £26,675 | £22,408 | £15,806 |

## Question 16

The year before 2011, Legal occupations earned 13% less than the average salary for 2011. What was the average salary for 2010?

| A | B | C | D | E |
|---|---|---|---|---|
| £33,558 | £38,367 | £36,866 | £33,867 | £34,568 |

*There are a total of 289 children with signs of ADHD.*

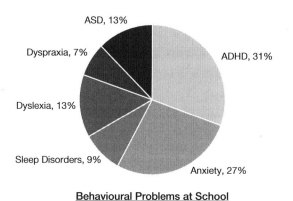

Behavioural Problems at School

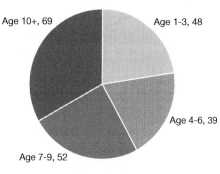

ADHD (Not clinically proven)

# Question 17

How many children are in this study?

| A | B | C | D | E |
|---|---|---|---|---|
| 912 | 972 | 952 | 932 | 942 |

# Question 18

What percentage of children with ADHD have not been clinically proven?

| A | B | C | D | E |
|---|---|---|---|---|
| 63% | 72% | 74% | 64% | 36% |

# Question 19

There are 21 children aged 4-6 with Dyslexia. What percentage of this behaviour problem does this represent?

| A | B | C | D | E |
|---|---|---|---|---|
| 19% | 21% | 35% | 32% | 17% |

# Question 20

If 11 per cent of Sleeping Disorders are found in age 7-9 year olds, how many children that age has a sleeping disorder?

| A | B | C | D | E |
|---|---|---|---|---|
| 10 | 11 | 7 | 9 | 5 |

# ANSWERS TO NUMERICAL REASONING – SUBSECTION 3

**Q1.** B

EXPLANATION = 150 (euros) x 0.78 (pounds sterling) = £117.

**Q2.** C

EXPLANATION = 70 x 0.02 = $1.4.

**Q3.** D

EXPLANATION = 100 / 0.55 = 181    140 / 0.87 = 160    181 – 160 = 21 (Canadian dollars).

**Q4.** E

EXPLANATION = 150 x 1.59 = 238.5    100 x 1.24 = 124.     238.5 – 124 = $114.50.

**Q5.** D

EXPLANATION = to work out the difference, add up the first 5 months for granite stone (18 + 25 + 28 + 31 + 40 = 142). Add up the first 5 months for marble stone (19 + 17 + 35 + 31 + 23 = 125). So, the difference between granite stone and marble stone imports = 17 (thousands).

**Q6.** C

EXPLANATION = the highest increase was between February and March. February's total = 63, March's total = 88. The difference is 25, no other months have a higher increased number.

**Q7.** A

EXPLANATION: 152:161. For the exact ratio, you need to find a number that goes in to both of these numbers. No other numbers (apart from 1 and itself can go into it). So, the answer would be 152:161.

**Q8.** C

EXPLANATION: 170 / 483 x 100 = 35.19. Rounded up to 1 decimal place = 35.2.

**Q9.** B

EXPLANATION = 375,995 – 325,000 = 50,995    50,995 / 325,000 x 100 = 15.69 = 15.7%.

**Q10.** C

EXPLANATION = Company C was the furthest away from their target by £234,250.

**Q11.** D

EXPLANATION = 420,000 – 275,000 = 145,000     145,000 / 420,000 x 100 = 34.5%.

**Q12.** A

EXPLANATION = 375,995 / 100 x 123 = 462,473.85 = £462,474.

**Q13.** E

EXPLANATION = 42,716 / 100 x 113 = £48,269.

**Q14.** B

EXPLANATION = 37,804 / 100 x 90 = 34,024.

**Q15.** C

EXPLANATION = 54,470 / 100 x 107 = 58,282.9   35,515 / 100 x 89 = 31,608.35
58,282.9 – 31,608.35 = 26,674.55. To the nearest whole number = £26,675.

**Q16.** D

EXPLANATION = 38,270 x 100 / 113 = 33,867.

**Q17.** D

EXPLANATION = 289 (not clinically proven) x 100 / 31 (percentage of people with ADHD) = 932.

**Q18.** B

EXPLANATION = 208 / 289 x 100 = 71.97%. Nearest whole number = 72%.

**Q19.** E

EXPLANATION = 21 / 121 x 100 = 17.35. Nearest whole number 17%.

**Q20.** D

EXPLANATION = 932 / 100 x 9 = 83.44 (Rounded up = 84). 84 / 100 x 11 = 9.24 (Rounded up = 9).

# NUMERICAL REASONING TESTS

## (SUBSECTION 4)

*The number of times a die was cast and the number of times
each individual number appeared*

| Casts | 1 | 2 | 3 | 4 | 5 | 6 |
|---|---|---|---|---|---|---|
| First 10 | 2 | 3 | 1 | 1 | 2 | 1 |
| First 20 | 5 | 4 | 3 | 4 | 3 | 1 |
| First 30 | 8 | 5 | 6 | 5 | 4 | 2 |
| First 40 | 10 | 6 | 7 | 6 | 5 | 6 |
| First 50 | 13 | 7 | 10 | 7 | 6 | 7 |

## Question 1

In no two consecutive casts did the same number appear. If the number 4 turned up in the 20th cast, which number/s could not have turned up in the 11th cast?

| A | B | C | D | E |
|---|---|---|---|---|
| 4 | 1 | 2 and 3 | 6 | 3 |

## Question 2

Which of the following numbers must have turned up the least amount of times in the first 50 casts?

| A | B | C | D | E |
|---|---|---|---|---|
| 2, 4 and 6 | 6 | 5 | 3 | 1 |

## Question 3

If the same number occurred for the 43rd cast and the 47th cast, what number/s could it be?

| A | B | C | D | E |
|---|---|---|---|---|
| 1 | 2 | 4 | 1 and 3 | 6 |

## Question 4

What is the total ratio of the number of 3's cast and the number of 5's cast? In its simplest terms.

| A | B | C | D | E |
|---|---|---|---|---|
| 10:13 | 5:3 | 7:10 | 10:6 | 3:5 |

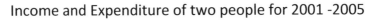

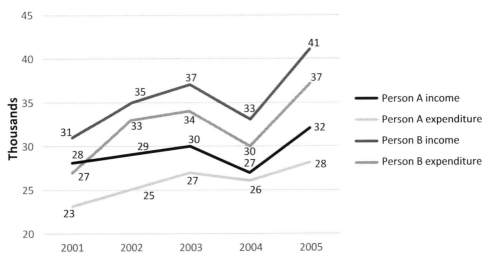

Income and Expenditure of two people for 2001 -2005

## Question 5

In how many years is the income for Person A less than that of the income for Person B?

| A | B | C | D | E |
|---|---|---|---|---|
| 1 | 2 | 3 | 4 | 5 |

## Question 6

How much profit (in thousands) does Person B have over the 5 year period?

| A | B | C | D | E |
|---|---|---|---|---|
| 13 | 21 | 16 | 19 | 8 |

## Question 7

In the following year of 2006, Person A earns 27% more than he did back in 2001. How much income does Person A make in 2006?

| A | B | C | D | E |
|---|---|---|---|---|
| £35,560 | £32,120 | £38,250 | £33,750 | £39,650 |

## Question 8

In the following year of 2006, Person B earns 11% less than he did in 2005. How much does Person B earn in 2006?

| A | B | C | D | E |
|---|---|---|---|---|
| £33,220 | £36,490 | £27,460 | £23,275 | £29,775 |

*Representation of the grades students achieved across five subjects*

| | English | Maths | Science | History | Media | | Grade | Pass Mark |
|---|---|---|---|---|---|---|---|---|
| David | A- | B+ | C- | C+ | B+ | | A+ | 96-100 |
| Billy | C- | C+ | B+ | A+ | A | | A | 91-95 |
| Elliott | B+ | B- | A+ | A- | C | | A- | 86-90 |
| Taralyn | C+ | B+ | B+ | C+ | A+ | | B+ | 81-85 |
| Alecia | C | C+ | A- | B- | C+ | | B | 76-80 |
| James | B- | B+ | C- | C+ | C | | B- | 71-75 |
| Gareth | B+ | B- | A | B- | C- | | C+ | 65-70 |
| Duncan | B- | C- | C+ | C- | C | | C | 59-64 |
| Joe | B+ | B | B | C | A | | C- | 50-58 |

## Question 9

Find the minimum possible of total marks for all nine candidates in Science.

| A | B | C | D | E |
|---|---|---|---|---|
| 507 | 776 | 667 | 676 | None of these |

## Question 10

What is the highest mark across all five subjects that David could have got?

| A | B | C | D | E |
|---|---|---|---|---|
| 298 | 386 | 320 | 408 | None of these |

## Question 11

What would Gareth's total average mark be, if he had scored the average mark in all his subjects?

| A | B | C | D | E |
|---|---|---|---|---|
| 78 | 75.2 | 76.2 | 79.4 | 76.5 |

## Question 12

If everyone scored the lowest pass mark in each subject, who scored the best overall?

| A | B | C | D | E |
|---|---|---|---|---|
| David | Taralyn | Alecia | Elliott | Joe |

*There are a total of 889 students in the Law Faculty*

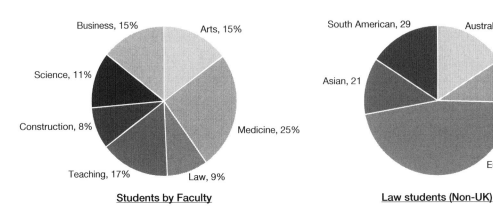

Students by Faculty      Law students (Non-UK)

## Question 13

How many students are there at the university?

| A | B | C | D | E |
|---|---|---|---|---|
| 8977 | 8979 | 9879 | 9788 | 9877 |

## Question 14

What percentage of the students in the Law faculty are Non-UK students?

| A | B | C | D | E |
|---|---|---|---|---|
| 15% | 35% | 20% | 40% | 70% |

## Question 15

If 14 percent of Construction students are European, how many European students are there studying Construction?

| A | B | C | D | E |
|---|---|---|---|---|
| 95 | 110 | 135 | 150 | 170 |

## Question 16

There are 364 European students studying Business. What percentage of the faculty does this represent?

| A | B | C | D | E |
|---|---|---|---|---|
| 5% | 15% | 50% | 35% | 25% |

*Electrical usage comparison for a company in 1990 and 2010*

| Company Departments | Company Electrical usage in 1990 | Company Electrical usage in 2010 |
|---|---|---|
| Finance | 12% | 14% |
| Marketing | 12% | 14% |
| Sales | 20% | 21% |
| Management | 15% | 12% |
| IT | 41% | 39% |
| | TOTAL = 18,000 kWh | TOTAL = 16,000 kWh |

## Question 17

Combining both Finance and IT departments, what was the difference in electrical usage from 1990 to 2010.

| A | B | C | D | E |
|---|---|---|---|---|
| 106 kWh | 86 kWh | 1060 kWh | 103 kWh | Cannot say |

## Question 18

In 2014, the electrical use is 8% higher than the usage in 2010 for the Sales department. What is the Sales department's electrical usage?

| A | B | C | D | E |
|---|---|---|---|---|
| 3826.6 kWh | 2236.8 kWh | 3336.8 kWh | 3862.8 kWh | 3628.8 kWh |

## Question 19

How much electricity did the Management department use in 2010?

| A | B | C | D | E |
|---|---|---|---|---|
| 1350 kWh | 1920 kWh | 1560 kWh | 1870 kWh | 1400 kWh |

## Question 20

What is the difference between the electrical usages for Marketing in 1990 compared to their use in 2010?

| A | B | C | D | E |
|---|---|---|---|---|
| 80 kWh | 110 kWh | 115 kWh | 5 kWh | 180 kWh |

# ANSWERS TO NUMERICAL REASONING – SUBSECTION 4

### Q1. D

EXPLANATION = the question may seem tricky at first, but if you notice, the individual number of 6 was cast once in the first 10 attempts, and only once in the first 20 attempts. Therefore, the number 6 could not have turned up from casts 11 – 20.

### Q2. C

EXPLANATION = the number 5 only appears 6 times in the first 50 casts, no other number has a lower cast rate at the end of 50 casts, therefore 5 is the number with the least amount of casts in 50 attempts.

### Q3. D

EXPLANATION = the numbers have to occur more than once between 40 and 50. Only the numbers 1 and 3 do this, therefore this would be the correct answer.

### Q4. B

EXPLANATION = total number of 3's cast = 10, total number of 5's cast = 6. Ratio would be 10:6 but, this would be wrong because it asks you to put it in its simplest terms, therefore you need to find a number that goes into both 10 and 6, which would 2. So, 10 / 2 = 5 and 6 / 2 = 3. Therefore, the answer would be = 5:3.

### Q5. E

EXPLANATION = Person A has a lower income for every year on the graph compared to the income for Person B, therefore the answer would be 5 years.

### Q6. C

EXPLANATION = 2001 = 31 – 27 = 4, 2002 = 35 – 33 = 2, 2003 = 37 – 34 = 3, 2004 = 33 – 30 = 3, 2005 = 41 – 37 = 4. So, 4 + 2 + 3 + 3 + 4 = 16 (thousands).

### Q7. A

EXPLANATION = 28,000 / 100 x 127(%) = £35,560.

### Q8. B

EXPLANATION = 41,000 / 100 x 89 = £36,490.

**Q9.** D

EXPLANATION = 50 + 81 + 96 + 81 + 86 + 50 + 91 + 65 + 76 = 676.

**Q10.** E

EXPLANATION = 90 + 85 + 58 + 70 + 85 = 388. None of the answers match, so therefore the answer must be 'none'.

**Q11.** B

EXPLANATION = average marks across all subjects = 83 + 73 + 93 + 73 + 54 = 376. Total average mark = 376 / 5 = 75.2.

**Q12.** D

EXPLANATION = Elliott's total if he scored the lowest in all the grade boundaries = 393. Nobody else scored a higher mark.

**Q13.** E

EXPLANATION = 889 / 100 x 9 = 9877. The answer is rounded to the nearest whole person.

**Q14.** C

EXPLANATION = 178 / 889 x 100 = 20.02% = 20%.

**Q15.** B

EXPLANATION = 9877 x (8/100) = 790. (790/100) x 14 = 110.

**Q16.** E

EXPLANATION = 9877 x (15/100) = 1482. (364/1482) x 100 = 24.56% = 25%.

**Q17.** C

EXPLANATION = 53% of 18,000 = 9540. 53% of 16,000 = 8480. So the decrease = 9540 – 8480 = 1060 kWh.

**Q18.** E

EXPLANATION = 21% of 16,000 = 3360. So, 3360 / 100 x 108 = 3628.8.

**Q19.** B

EXPLANATION = 16,000 / 100 x 12 = 1920.

**Q20.** A

EXPLANATION = 18,000 / 100 x 12 = 2160.    16,000 / 100 x 14 = 2240. So, 2240 – 2160 = 80 kWh.

# NUMERICAL REASONING TESTS

## (SUBSECTION 5)

| Currency | Pounds Sterling exchange rate 2013 | Percentage change from 2013 to 2014 |
|---|---|---|
| US dollars | 1:0.661 | 6% |
| Euro | 1:0.624 | -3% |
| Australian dollar | 1:0.598 | -8% |
| Canadian dollar | 1:0.606 | 8% |
| Russian Ruble | 1:0.621 | 2% |

## Question 1

How much would you get if you were to change up 127 US dollars into Pounds Sterling?

| A | B | C | D | E |
|---|---|---|---|---|
| £108.30 | £93.20 | £58.76 | £81.76 | £83.95 |

## Question 2

What is the new exchange rate for Australian dollars to Pounds Sterling?

| A | B | C | D | E |
|---|---|---|---|---|
| 1:0.621 | 1:0.224 | 1:0.315 | 1:0.550 | 1:0.440 |

## Question 3

How many Pounds Sterling would you receive if you were to change up 130 Canadian dollars after the new exchange rate?

| A | B | C | D | E |
|---|---|---|---|---|
| £83.75 | £81.05 | £85.02 | £87.06 | £84.01 |

## Question 4

What currency has the better exchange rate after the percentage change from 2013?

| A | B | C | D | E |
|---|---|---|---|---|
| US dollars | Euro | Australian dollars | Canadian dollars | Russian Ruble |

| Job sectors | Number of male employees | Number of female employees |
|---|---|---|
| Finance | 33,000 | 27,000 |
| Business | 192,000 | 108,000 |
| Legal | 87,000 | 79,000 |
| Media | 103,000 | 112,000 |
| Medicine | 213,000 | 197,000 |
| Self-employed | 117,000 | 64,000 |
| Unemployed | 41,000 | 56,000 |
| TOTALS = | 786,000 | 643,000 |

## Question 5

Approximately, what percentage of the people sampled are self-employed? To the nearest whole number.

| A | B | C | D | E |
|---|---|---|---|---|
| 9% | 11% | 21% | 13% | 7% |

## Question 6

The number of female employees in the Legal sector increases by 18%. How many female employees would there be in the Legal sector after this increase?

| A | B | C | D | E |
|---|---|---|---|---|
| 95,400 | 93,220 | 97,440 | 98,105 | 104,020 |

## Question 7

The number of male medical employees is 213,000. In the following year, this decreases by 11%. The year after that sees an increase by 20% of the previous year. How many male medical employees are there now?

| A | B | C | D | E |
|---|---|---|---|---|
| 255,600 | 227,484 | 232,170 | 214,590 | 268,750 |

## Question 8

In its simplest form, what is the ratio of unemployed male to female employees?

| A | B | C | D | E |
|---|---|---|---|---|
| 4:5 | 41:59 | 41:56 | 82:112 | 39:56 |

| PROD-UCT | No. of units sold (1000's) | Cost of material per unit (£) | Manu-facturing costs per unit (£) | Total cost per unit (£) | Sales price per unit (£) | Total Sales Revenue (£) |
|---|---|---|---|---|---|---|
| P | 18.5 | 2.25 | 2.15 | 4.4 | 6.5 | 38,850 |
| Q | 29.5 | 4.75 | 2.25 | 7 | 10 | ? |
| R | 9 | 1.5 | 1.75 | 3.25 | 8 | 42,750 |
| S | 13 | 3.5 | 2.25 | 5.75 | 15 | 120,250 |

## Question 9

Calculate the total sales revenue for product Q.

| A | B | C | D | E |
|---|---|---|---|---|
| £36,500 | £80,800 | £88,500 | £81,250 | £85,750 |

## Question 10

For the following year, product R sells triple the amount shown in this table. What would the total sales revenue be?

| A | B | C | D | E |
|---|---|---|---|---|
| £48,750 | £110,250 | £120,258 | £135,750 | £128,250 |

## Question 11

Which product is making the most profits per unit?

| A | B | C | D | E |
|---|---|---|---|---|
| Product P | Product Q | Product R | Product S | Product Q and S |

## Question 12

Product P gets taxed 25% of the total sales revenue. What would the total sales revenue be after tax?

| A | B | C | D | E |
|---|---|---|---|---|
| £23,126.75 | £28,215.25 | £29,137.50 | £30,100.05 | £27,251.25 |

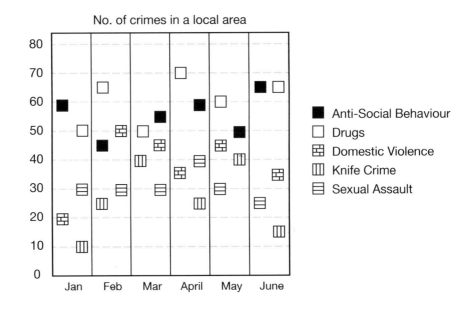

No. of crimes in a local area

## Question 13

What month was drug-related crime at its highest?

| A | B | C | D | E |
|---|---|---|---|---|
| January | February | March | April | May |

## Question 14

What percentage of the total number of crimes were drug-related?

| A | B | C | D | E |
|---|---|---|---|---|
| 23% | 17% | 8% | 31% | 28% |

## Question 15

How many knife crimes occurred in June?

| A | B | C | D | E |
|---|---|---|---|---|
| 15 | 30 | 45 | 60 | 80 |

## Question 16

In what month was Anti-Social Behaviour and drug crime the same?

| A | B | C | D | E |
|---|---|---|---|---|
| June | May | April | March | February |

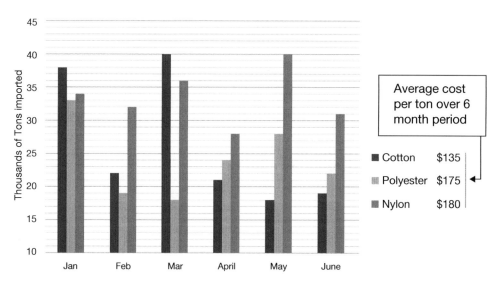

The above table shows imports for three different materials. Use this information to answer the following questions. Please circle the correct answer.

## Question 17

What is the mean value for nylon imports over the six month period?

| A | B | C | D | E |
|---|---|---|---|---|
| 42.5 | 18.5 | 33.5 | 49.5 | 37.5 |

## Question 18

What was the difference in thousands of tons between cotton material and nylon material in the first 3 months?

| A | B | C | D | E |
|---|---|---|---|---|
| 5 | 15 | 24 | 17 | 2 |

## Question 19

What was the ratio of polyester to nylon material in the first 4 months?

| A | B | C | D | E |
|---|---|---|---|---|
| 12:3 | 47:65 | 17:13 | 11:7 | 9.5 |

## Question 20

Which month showed the largest total increase in imports compared to the previous month?

| A | B | C | D | E |
|---|---|---|---|---|
| June | February | April | March | January |

# ANSWERS TO NUMERICAL REASONING – SUBSECTION 5

**Q1.** E

EXPLANATION = 127 x 0.661 = 83.95.

**Q2.** D

EXPLANATION = 0.598 / 100 x 92 = 0.550.

**Q3.** C

EXPLANATION = 0.606 / 100 x 108 = 0.654. So, 130 x 0.654 = 85.02.

**Q4.** A

EXPLANATION = US dollars = 0.661 / 10 x 6 = 0.700. Euro = 0.624 / 100 x 97 = 0.605. Australian dollars = 0.598 / 100 x 92 = 0.550. Canadian dollars = 0.606 / 100 x 108 = 0.654. Russian Ruble = 0.621 / 100 x 102 = 0.633. So the highest exchange rate is US dollars.

**Q5.** D

EXPLANATION = 117,000 + 64,000 = 181,000.   786,000 + 643,000 = 1,429,000. So, 181,000 / 1,429,000 x 100 = 12.66%. To the nearest whole number = 13%.

**Q6.** B

EXPLANATION = 79,000 / 100 x 118 = 93,220.

**Q7.** B

EXPLANATION = 213,000 / 100 x 89 = 189,570. 189,570 / 100 x 120 = 227,484.

**Q8.** C

EXPLANATION = 41,000:56,000. Both numbers can be divided by 1,000 = 41:56.

**Q9.** C

EXPLANATION = 10 – 7 = 3 x 29.5 (thousands) = 88,500.

**Q10.** E

EXPLANATION = 42,750 x 3 = 128,250.

**Q11.** D

EXPLANATION = the sales price per unit = 15. The total cost to produce the product = 5.75. 15 - 5.75 = 9.25. Therefore, they are making a profit of 9.25.

**Q12.** C

EXPLANATION = 38,850 / 100 x 25 = 9712.5. So 38,850 – 9712.50 = 29,137.50.

**Q13.** D

EXPLANATION = April had the highest number of drug crimes with 70 incidents.

**Q14.** E

EXPLANATION = total number of crimes = 1265. Number of drug-related crimes = 360. So, 360 / 1265 x 100 = 28%.

**Q15.** A

EXPLANATION = the number of knife crimes in June = 15.

**Q16.** A

EXPLANATION = June saw the same number of drug crimes and ASB with each incident occurring 65 times in the month.

**Q17.** C

EXPLANATION = 34 + 32 + 36 + 28 + 40 + 31 = 201 / 6 = 33.5.

**Q18.** E

EXPLANATION = add up the first 3 months for cotton (38 + 22 + 40 = 100). Add up the first 3 months for nylon (34 + 32 + 36 = 102). So, the difference be¬tween cotton and nylon = 2 (thousands).

**Q19.** B

EXPLANATION =  Total for Polyester = 94,000. Total for Nylon = 13,000. Divide both numbers by 2000 to give you 47:65.

**Q20.** D

EXPLANATION = the highest increase was between February and March. February's total = 73, March's total = 94. The difference is 21, no other months have a higher increased number.

# CHAPTER 5

# *VERBAL REASONING TESTS*

## *(SUBSECTION 1)*

For the verbal reasoning tests, Fast Stream candidates will be provided with a written passage which they must read carefully in order to answer the following questions.

For the real test, it will comprise of 40 questions which should be completed in approximately 20 minutes. However, this chapter will provide you with lots of practice questions for you to work through. We have deliberately chosen to do this so you are fully prepared before your real test.

Before you begin this testing section, let's take a look at the below example:

# EXAMPLE

## Passage

Many organisations find it useful to employee students over the summer period. A lot of permanent staff like to take their holidays over this period, especially if they have children. Companies need to maintain a solid workforce over this period because it usually peaks in terms of business. Giving students the opportunity for part time work over the summer could result in a more permanent position after their education. Unlike permanent staff, students working on a part time basis are not eligible for holiday pay or bonus incentives.

## Statement

Some companies need to recruit part time staff over the summer because they have more work to do.

**True, False, or Impossible to say?**

## How to work it out

The statement already mentions that 'some' companies experience their 'peak' times over the summer, therefore the statement would be true.

## Answer

True

You will experience similar verbal reasoning questions on your fast stream tests. The following pages contain 100 verbal reasoning practice questions, each with an explanation to obtain the answer. The answers and explanations can be found at the end of every sub-section.

We have deliberately not provided you with a time limit. This will allow you to work through these questions carefully and at a pace that suits you.

Please write your answer in the answer box provided.

## PASSAGE 1

The case of a Mumbai couple who approached the courts in India after their time limit for an abortion was overdue, wanted a termination of their pregnancy. This case of euthanasia was denied by the courts. The parents wanted to be granted permission for termination of their pregnancy after they found out that the foetus had been damaged and detected to have possible disabilities which would affect the life of the unborn child. The courts however, argued that the unborn child has the right to live despite being possibly disabled.

## Question 1

The courts in India have the right and authority to sanction euthanasia.

A – True

B – False

C – Impossible to say

Answer

## Question 2

The courts believe that the child has no rights because it is unborn.

A – True

B – False

C – Impossible to say

Answer

## Question 3

If the Mumbai couple continue with their pregnancy, it will cause health risks to both mother and baby.

A – True

B – False

C – Impossible to say

Answer [                    ]

## Question 4

The courts consider how far along a woman is in her pregnancy before granting permission for euthanasia.

A – True

B – False

C – Impossible to say

Answer [                    ]

## Question 5

If the woman was to give birth to her child, her child would grow up with a disability.

A – True

B – False

C – Impossible to say

Answer [                    ]

## PASSAGE 2

The Chinese Government implemented a policy in the late 1970's to address and reduce the country's birth rate. The Government decided to introduce a one-child policy to create better access to education and health benefits. However, in recent years the one-child policy has become somewhat 're-laxed'. Chinese citizens are now able to apply to have a second child if their first child was a girl, or if both parents were an only-child. In 2008, China's population slowly increased to 1.3 billion.

## Question 6

Previous Chinese Governments had discouraged people to have large families.

A – True

B – False

C – Impossible to say

Answer

## Question 7

In 2007, China's population was more than 1.3 billion.

A – True

B – False

C – Impossible to say

Answer

## Question 8

In the passage, it is concluded that the one-child policy was implemented to ensure Chinese citizens with a better lifestyle.

A – True

B – False

C – Impossible to say

Answer

## Question 9

Women were made to have an abortion if they got pregnant again after their first child.

A – True

B – False

C – Impossible to say

Answer

## Question 10

The one-child policy is strict and inflexible to ensure China's population is maintained.

A – True

B – False

C – Impossible to say

Answer

## PASSAGE 3

The Sexual Harassment of Women in the Workplace Act 2013 was amended by the lower courts in India to ensure women's rights were protected against sexual harassment. This will help to contribute to gender equality, liberty and equity. The Act was implemented after a group of women (known as Vishaka) filed a petition after a woman was brutally raped for stopping a child marriage. This case caused a set of procedural guidelines to be created, known as the Vishaka guidelines, and now used for any sexual harassment case.

## Question 11

India had no policies or procedures in place to deal with sexual harassment in the workplace before the case of Vishaka.

A – True

B – False

C – Impossible to say

Answer

## Question 12

In the passage, it concludes that the Vishaka guidelines was the reason for the amendment of the sexual harassment Act.

A – True

B – False

C – Impossible to say

Answer

## Question 13

There was no gender equality before this sexual harassment Act was implemented.

A – True

B – False

C – Impossible to say

Answer

## Question 14

India has more problems regarding sexual harassment in the workplace compared to other developing countries.

A – True

B – False

C – Impossible to say

Answer

## Question 15

Many organisations will become more profitable as a result of implementing the sexual harassment Act.

A – True

B – False

C – Impossible to say

Answer

# PASSAGE 4

Child trafficking is a form of child abuse. Children are often recruited and then transported and exploited. Children are trafficked to provide benefit fraud, sexual abuse, forced marriage or criminal activity. Child trafficking is a global crime and cannot always be spotted; there is no single piece of legislation in regards to trafficking in the UK. However, there are some legislations that cover areas which trafficking falls under. In order to address this issue, we need to address global, social and economic inequality and improve awareness and understanding. We need to reduce the demand for trafficked children and make the 'business' an unprofitable one.

## Question 16

In the passage, it is concluded that there is no single way to tackle child trafficking.

A – True

B – False

C – Impossible to say

Answer

## Question 17

Child trafficking has become increasingly popular in the UK.

A – True

B – False

C – Impossible to say

Answer

## Question 18

In the passage, it can be concluded that the hidden nature of child trafficking makes it extremely difficult to identify its victims, to identify the scale of the problem and to develop an effective and life-changing response.

A – True

B – False

C – Impossible to say

Answer

## Question 19

Tackling sexual abuse in regards to children will prevent children from being trafficked.

A – True

B – False

C – Impossible to say

Answer

## Question 20

Child trafficking is a 'profitable' business.

A – True

B – False

C – Impossible to say

Answer

# ANSWERS TO VERBAL REASONING TESTS – SUBSECTION 1

**Q1.** A, True

EXPLANATION = the couple went to the courts in India because they wanted a termination of their pregnancy. Thus, the courts must be able to sanction euthanasia, and therefore this would be true.

**Q2.** B, False

EXPLANATION = in the passage, it clearly states that the courts argued that "the unborn child has the right to live despite being possibly disabled". Therefore the statement contradicts this and so it must be false.

**Q3.** C, Impossible to say

EXPLANATION = although the passage indicates problems with the foetus and that it has been detected of carrying disabilities, the passage does not mention anything about causing any harm to mother and baby during the pregnancy, therefore it is impossible to make this conclusion.

**Q4.** C, Impossible to say

EXPLANATION = although you could assume that the courts take into consideration how far along a woman is in her pregnancy, it is not indicated anywhere in the passage, and so this statement cannot be concluded.

**Q5.** C, Impossible to say

EXPLANATION = it is impossible to say for definite whether or not the child would have a disability. The passage indicates that the foetus has been damaged and therefore "possible disabilities" may affect the child. It is not definite, therefore you cannot make this conclusion based on the information provided.

**Q6.** B, False

EXPLANATION = if previous Chinese Governments had prevented citizens from having larger families, there wouldn't be a need to implement new policies to help reduce China's population. Therefore this is most probably false.

**Q7.** B, False

EXPLANATION = this statement would be false. In the passage, it states that in 2008 "China's population slowly increased to 1.3 billion". Therefore, in 2007, the population would have been somewhat lower than 1.3 billion.

**Q8.** A, True

EXPLANATION = the policy was implemented to ensure better access to education and healthcare benefits, therefore ensures citizens of a better life-style, thus the statement must be true.

**Q9.** B, False

EXPLANATION = the fact that they can apply to have another child indicates that women were not made to have an abortion and therefore this statement would be false.

**Q10.** B, False

EXPLANATION = the fact that they can apply to have another child demonstrates that the one-child policy is not strict or inflexible, it is purely there as a measuring tool, which does offer some flexibility.

**Q11.** C, Impossible to say

EXPLANATION = although the passage states that this Act was implemented in 2013, you are not told whether there were any Acts serving for women's rights against sexual harassment prior to this. Therefore, you cannot make this conclusion.

**Q12.** B, False

EXPLANATION = the Vishaka guidelines were the result of the sexual harassment Act being implemented, it wasn't the cause. The cause itself was the group of women who filed the petition, which led to the guidelines being made.

**Q13.** C, Impossible to say

EXPLANATION = it is impossible to conclude from the statement whether there were any policies in place for gender equality. The passage indicates this Act would help to 'contribute' to gender equality, therefore suggesting it's already being assessed, but this is an assumption and therefore you cannot make this conclusion.

**Q14.** C, Impossible to say

EXPLANATION = there is no way of knowing whether India has more issues regarding sexual harassment compared to other developing countries. The passage does not mention any statistics, nor does it mention other countries, so it is impossible to say.

**Q15.** C, Impossible to say

EXPLANATION = it is impossible to say whether organisations will become more profitable. It is unlikely that a sexual harassment act will have any effect on a company's profits, but the passage does not give you enough information to rule this out, therefore you simply cannot say.

**Q16.** A, True

EXPLANATION = the passage clearly indicates that there is no single piece of legislation to tackle child trafficking. Nor is there a single way to reduce child trafficking.

**Q17.** C, Impossible to say

EXPLANATION = the passage does not mention anything about the frequency in which child trafficking goes on in the UK, therefore you cannot make this conclusion.

**Q18.** A, True

EXPLANATION = after reading the passage it is true to say that it is difficult to identify its victims ("cannot always be spotted"), identify the scale ("global issue"), and develop effective responses ("address global social and economic inequality and improve awareness and understanding"). Therefore this conclusion can be made.

**Q19.** C, Impossible to say

EXPLANATION = it is impossible to say whether tackling sexual abuse will prevent children from being trafficked. This is unlikely going to make a difference. Children are trafficked for other reasons, so it would be impractical to say this would eliminate the problem.

**Q20.** A, True

EXPLANATION = in the passage it states that we need to reduce the demand for trafficked children and make the 'business' an unprofitable one. Therefore the statement must be true, not just in terms of money but by other means as well.

# VERBAL
# REASONING TESTS

## (SUBSECTION 2)

## PASSAGE 1

A local shopkeeper was giving a statement to the police in regards to a robbery on his shop. He stated that as he was closing up the shop at approximately 23:45, when a person entered the door. He had his back towards the person and said "Sorry, we're closed!" A few seconds later, the person scarpered to the tills demanding money. The person was wearing a balaclava, and the only lights that were on were the ones shining in from the street lamps outside. The shopkeeper opened up the till and the money was scooped up.

### Question 1

The robber was a man.

A – True

B – False

C – Impossible to say

Answer

### Question 2

The shopkeeper scooped up the money and handed it to the robber.

A – True

B – False

C – Impossible to say

Answer

## Question 3

Only three people saw what happened in the shop that night.

A – True

B – False

C – Impossible to say

Answer

## Question 4

The lights in the shop were switched off.

A – True

B – False

C – Impossible to say

Answer

## Question 5

The robber escaped with the money.

A – True

B – False

C – Impossible to say

Answer

## PASSAGE 2

Employees working in an organisation are bound by confidentiality. They have a duty to keep information, data and any work-related issues quiet. Severe consequences are often a result of breaking the confidentiality agreement. Employers issue confidentially agreement contracts whereby both parties need to sign the clause and agree to the terms and conditions.

### Question 6

If suspension is a possible 'severe consequence' for employers to use, then employees who break the confidentiality agreement may be at risk of being suspended.

A – True

B – False

C – Impossible to say

Answer

### Question 7

Mentors of groups of employees are subject to dismissal if they do not prevent employees from leaking information.

A – True

B – False

C – Impossible to say

Answer

## Question 8

Discretion is part of their binding contract with their employers.

A – True

B – False

C – Impossible to say

Answer [ ]

## Question 9

Organisations use the same punishment methods for employees who do not comply with the rules of the company.

A – True

B – False

C – Impossible to say

Answer [ ]

## Question 10

In the passage, it is concluded that telling someone outside the working environment about data you may have found, is acceptable, in order to get a third party point of view.

A – True

B – False

C – Impossible to say

Answer [ ]

## PASSAGE 3

Child labour has and probably always will be a significant global issue associated with poverty, inadequate education, lack of opportunity and a range of health problems. Developing countries such as Asia, Africa and Latin America are amongst the biggest countries in which child labour is at its highest. Child labour can be used to create workers from an early age and get paid very little, if any. Such working conditions jeopardise children's health and lifestyles. They are made to work at a very young age, are malnourished and work long hours in unpleasant working conditions.

## Question 11

Child labour is only occurring in developing countries and not countries that are already developed.

A – True

B – False

C – Impossible to say

Answer [          ]

## Question 12

Less developed countries use child labour as a way of maintaining workforces.

A – True

B – False

C – Impossible to say

Answer [          ]

## Question 13

Child labour is a way of exploiting children.

A – True

B – False

C – Impossible to say

Answer [            ]

## Question 14

The majority of child labour goes on in Asia.

A – True

B – False

C – Impossible to say

Answer [            ]

## Question 15

In the passage, it is concluded that child labour is a global problem that continues to exist in today's society.

A – True

B – False

C – Impossible to say

Answer [            ]

## PASSAGE 4

Recent research suggests that candidates face an 88% job rejection if their CV includes a photo of themselves. The exponential growth of social media platforms and personal profiles are frequently considered by many employers in the job recruitment process. It is argued by many that making CV's anonymous will benefit everyone, including employers. It will give everyone the same equal chance to apply for a job without personal mannerisms getting in the way. Name, gender, photographs, race etc, should all be removed so candidates can be assessed purely on skill, experience and performance.

## Question 16

In the passage, it is concluded that minimising discrimination would ensure equality amongst individuals.

A – True

B – False

C – Impossible to say

Answer [                    ]

## Question 17

Only 12% of employers reject CV's if they have a photo attached.

A – True

B – False

C – Impossible to say

Answer [                    ]

## Question 18

Employers base their decisions on employing candidates solely on reading their social media and personal profiles.

A – True

B – False

C – Impossible to say

Answer

## Question 19

Photos, gender, name and race are all ways in which employers can discriminate against someone.

A – True

B – False

C – Impossible to say

Answer

## Question 20

If an employer selected a candidate who sent in their CV with a photo, the employer chose the candidate based on looks.

A – True

B – False

C – Impossible to say

Answer

# ANSWERS TO VERBAL REASONING TESTS – SUBSECTION 2

**Q1.** C, Impossible to say

EXPLANATION = the passage does not mention the gender of the robber, therefore you cannot make this assumption.

**Q2.** C, Impossible to say

EXPLANATION = the passage does not mention who picked up the money in the tills, it could have been the robber or the shopkeeper, therefore you cannot make this conclusion.

**Q3.** C, Impossible to say

EXPLANATION = you know there was the shopkeeper and the robber there that night, that makes two people who would have seen it. It is impossible to say from the passage provided whether anyone else saw what happened. Maybe someone saw something from outside. Therefore you cannot make this conclusion.

**Q4.** A, True

EXPLANATION = the passage states that the only light in the shop was coming from the street lamps outside, therefore this conclusion would be true.

**Q5.** C, Impossible to say

EXPLANATION = the passage does not mention whether or not the robber got away with the money. Therefore you cannot make this conclusion.

**Q6.** A, True

EXPLANATION = the passage states that breaking the confidentiality agreement can lead to 'severe consequences'. Thus, if suspension is one of those consequences, employers could use this as their punishment.

**Q7.** C, Impossible to say

EXPLANATION = you cannot say based on the information provided whether mentors also get punished if they know of employees who are breaking the confidentiality agreement. The passage does not mention repercussions in relation to "mentors", therefore you cannot make this conclusion.

**Q8.** A, True

EXPLANATION = the passage clearly indicates that both employees and employers are made to sign a contract to demonstrate their agreement in relation to confidential issues, therefore this conclusion is true.

**Q9.** C, Impossible to say

EXPLANATION = it is impossible to say based on the information provided whether all organisations use the same methods of punishing their employees. It is unlikely that they do, but you are given no information to support this, therefore you cannot say.

**Q10.** B, False

EXPLANATION = disclosing any information about something you are working on is not acceptable and breaks the confidentiality code of conduct. Therefore this conclusion is false.

**Q11.** C, Impossible to say

EXPLANATION = you cannot say based on the information provided whether child labour only occurs in developing countries. You are not given enough information to come to this conclusion, therefore it is impossible to say.

**Q12.** A, True

EXPLANATION = child labour is another way of saying that children are used to forcefully work. Therefore less developed countries use children as a way of maintaining their workforces, and so this statement must be true.

**Q13.** A, True

EXPLANATION = child labour is a way of making children work in unhealthy working conditions. They are exploited, and taken advantage of from a very early age, therefore this conclusion must be true.

**Q14.** C, Impossible to say

EXPLANATION = there is no way to indicate whether the majority of child labour goes in Asia. Although the passage states Asia as being one of the countries where child labour is at its highest, it does not mean to say it has the majority, you cannot compare it to other countries, and therefore you cannot make this conclusion.

**Q15.** A, True

EXPLANATION = from the passage it clearly indicates that child labour is a global issue and "has and probably always will be a significant problem". The fact that this statement says it 'has' and 'probably always will be' an issue demonstrates that child labour has existed in the past and will continue to exist in the future. Therefore, child labour must exist today and therefore the conclusion must be true.

**Q16.** A, True

EXPLANATION = the passage clearly demonstrates how equality should be a necessity for employment. Employers should base their decision on performance and skill, rather than looks or race. Therefore this conclusion is true.

**Q17.** B, False

EXPLANATION = the passage indicates that 88% of employers reject a job application if a photo is attached. The statement contradicts the passage and therefore is false.

**Q18.** C, Impossible to say

EXPLANATION = you cannot determine whether employers only employ people based on reading a candidates social media or personal profile. They may employ people because they are suitably qualified for the job. Therefore it is impossible to say this is the only reason.

**Q19.** A, True

EXPLANATION = the passage clearly indicates these examples as ways of showing how an employer can use them in the selection process of choosing employees, therefore this conclusion is true.

**Q20.** C, Impossible to say

EXPLANATION = it is impossible to say whether the employer based their decision on the photo that was attached to the person's CV. They may have chosen the candidate because they were the most suitable for the job role. Therefore it is impossible to say.

# VERBAL REASONING TESTS

## (SUBSECTION 3)

## PASSAGE 1

Many organisations find it useful to employee students over the summer period. A lot of permanent staff like to take their holidays over this period, especially if they have children. Companies need to maintain a solid workforce over this period because it usually peaks in terms of business. Giving students the opportunity for part time work over the summer could result in a more permanent position after their education. Unlike permanent staff, students working on a part time basis are not eligible for holiday pay or bonus incentives.

## Question 1

Organisations that do not recruit students over the summer, lose profits.

A – True

B – False

C – Impossible to say

Answer

## Question 2

It is possible that employees who wish to take their holidays during the summer can be covered by students.

A – True

B – False

C – Impossible to say

Answer

## Question 3

Students receive the same benefits as permanent staff.

A – True

B – False

C – Impossible to say

Answer

## Question 4

Offering part time work for students over the summer could lead to more opportunities.

A – True

B – False

C – Impossible to say

Answer

## Question 5

Companies rely on students working over the summer.

A – True

B – False

C – Impossible to say

Answer

## PASSAGE 2

In 2013, companies are increasingly expanding their presence on the web. Most companies believe that in order to succeed, they should devote more time in web designing and SEO. However, it is argued that companies are more likely to succeed if they pay more attention to data management and social networking. Using data management alongside social networking ensures maximum business potential and demonstrates the ability to run an effective and social networking system.

## Question 6

Only companies devoting their time in social networking and data management will succeed.

A – True

B – False

C – Impossible to say

Answer [              ]

## Question 7

No company is spending time on SEO and web design.

A – True

B – False

C – Impossible to say

Answer [              ]

## Question 8

Data management is more important than web designing.

A – True

B – False

C – Impossible to say

Answer

## Question 9

In the passage, it is concluded that the profits of a business can only be increased by using data management and social networking.

A – True

B – False

C – Impossible to say

Answer

## Question 10

In 2012, companies focused less on their presence on the web.

A – True

B – False

C – Impossible to say

Answer

## PASSAGE 3

When it comes to gun crime, America holds the top spot. The United States is said to have nearly twice as many guns per 100 people as the next highest, Yemen. America having 88.8 guns per 100 compared to 54.8 in Yemen. Guns are associated with more homicides across more industrialised countries. However, despite the level of gun crime and the number of people who have a gun, the murder rate is decreasing. This may be due to smarter policing methods, and the removal of toxins like lead in the environment. Whatever the factors, they are decreasing crime rate in relation to gun crime.

### Question 11

If you were to live in a more industrialised country, you will face more homicides in your area.

A – True

B – False

C – Impossible to say

Answer

### Question 12

In the passage, it is concluded that despite the number of people with guns in the United States, the murder rate in relation to gun crime is decreasing.

A – True

B – False

C – Impossible to say

Answer

## Question 13

Policing methods have become more advanced and therefore this could be a reason as to why the murder rate is decreasing.

A – True

B – False

C – Impossible to say

Answer

## Question 14

Out of 100 people, there are approximately 34 more guns in the United States compared to the guns in Yemen.

A – True

B – False

C – Impossible to say

Answer

## Question 15

People who have a gun are people who feel vulnerable and unprotected.

A – True

B – False

C – Impossible to say

Answer

## PASSAGE 4

Barristers play a vital role in the courts. Their work is advocacy – they present cases in courts. They are briefed by solicitors about the situation of a client's case. The barrister can take an independent judgement as to how to proceed with the case. Barristers provide specialist legal advice and make persuasive arguments which obtain the best possible result for the client. They need to be able to override the duty to assist the administration of justice.

### Question 16

It is the barrister who has the first interaction with the client.

A – True

B – False

C – Impossible to say

Answer [                    ]

### Question 17

The barrister has the role of implementing a structured and well versed argument to support the client's case to ensure the best possible outcome.

A – True

B – False

C – Impossible to say

Answer [                    ]

## Question 18

It is the barrister who has the final judgement of the case.

A – True

B – False

C – Impossible to say

Answer [                    ]

## Question 19

Barristers are the only professionals who deals with client cases in courts.

A – True

B – False

C – Impossible to say

Answer [                    ]

## Question 20

More people are needing the help of barristers to file a claim or issue in court.

A – True

B – False

C – Impossible to say

Answer [                    ]

# ANSWERS TO VERBAL REASONING TESTS – SUBSECTION 3

**Q1.** C, Impossible to say

EXPLANATION = it is impossible to say whether organisations would lose out on profits over the summer if they do not recruit students. Their profits may not be affected. You simply cannot say from the information provided.

**Q2.** A, True

EXPLANATION = the passage indicates that permanent staff can have their work taken over by students covering for them over the summer holidays. Therefore this statement must be true.

**Q3.** B, False

EXPLANATION = the passage clearly indicates that students are not eligible for holiday pay or bonus incentives, therefore they do not receive the same benefits as permanent staff, thus this statement is false.

**Q4.** A, True

EXPLANATION = the passage states that students working over the summer could result in a more permanent position. Therefore, this statement is true.

**Q5.** C, Impossible to say

EXPLANATION = it is impossible to say whether organisations rely on students working over the summer. The passage does not give you enough information to suggest this, therefore you cannot say.

**Q6.** C, Impossible to say

EXPLANATION = it is impossible to say whether companies will succeed only by using data management and social networking. Companies may use other ways to ensure business success, therefore you cannot make this judgement.

**Q7.** B, False

EXPLANATION = the passage clearly indicates that 'some' companies devote their time in web designing and SEO. Therefore this conclusion is false.

**Q8.** C, Impossible to say

EXPLANATION = you cannot tell whether data management is more important than web design. There is no evidence, statistics or information in the passage that allows you to draw that conclusion.

**Q9.** C, Impossible to say

EXPLANATION = the passage does not draw this conclusion. The passage does not mention anything about profits in relation to companies using data management and social networking.

**Q10.** A, True

EXPLANATION = the passage indicates that in 2013, companies were 'increasingly' becoming more focused on their presence of web design. So, in 2012, companies must have focused less on their presence on the web, therefore this conclusion must be true.

**Q11.** C, Impossible to say

EXPLANATION = it is impossible to say whether living in a more industrialised country will create more homicides in the area in which you live. You cannot tell whether this is true, so therefore you cannot say based on the information provided.

**Q12.** A, True

EXPLANATION = from the passage, it states that although there are more people with guns, the crime rate is lowering, so therefore this conclusion must be true.

**Q13.** A, True

EXPLANATION = the passage clearly indicates that policing methods could be a reason as to why the murder rate is declining, therefore the statement must be true.

**Q14.** A, True

EXPLANATION = the passage gives the figures of 88.8 and 54.8 to compare the number of guns in the United States and Yemen. Approximately the difference is 34, therefore the statement must be true.

**Q15.** C, Impossible to say

EXPLANATION = it is impossible to say why people have a gun. The passage does not mention anything about the reasons as to why people have a gun, therefore you cannot make this conclusion.

**Q16.** B, False

EXPLANATION = the passage clearly indicates that the solicitor is the person who briefs the barrister about the case, therefore the barrister is not the first person who is in contact with the client.

**Q17.** A, True

EXPLANATION = the passage clearly indicates that it is the role of the barrister who implements a structured view of how to proceed with the case to ensure the best possible results for the client. Therefore this conclusion is true.

**Q18.** C, Impossible to say

EXPLANATION = it is impossible to say whether the barrister has the final say in the decision making of a client's case. The passage does not mention anything about the final decision and who makes it. Therefore you cannot make this conclusion.

**Q19.** B, False

EXPLANATION = the passage clearly indicates that alongside barristers, solicitors play a role in the client's case in courts. Therefore, this statement must be false.

**Q20.** C, Impossible to say

EXPLANATION = it is impossible to say whether barristers are being used more in court cases because more people are going to court. The passage does not mention anything about barristers in relation to how much work they get or how many clients are filing a complaint. Therefore you simply cannot make this conclusion.

# VERBAL REASONING TESTS

## (SUBSECTION 4)

## PASSAGE 1

The influence of organisations over the last few years has indicated that the level of corporate social responsibility has dramatically increased. Social responsibility is a way of maintaining ethics, principles and integrity. Social responsibility affects a lot of aspects of our lives, such as working, human rights and the environment. The Government have a job to police unethical and corrupt behaviour in order to maintain a good standard of moral and social responsibility.

## Question 1

Corporate responsibilities have changed over the last few years.

A – True

B – False

C – Impossible to say

Answer

## Question 2

Social responsibility influences our lifestyles.

A – True

B – False

C – Impossible to say

Answer

## Question 3

The Government rely on large corporations to maintain high levels of corporate social responsibility.

A – True

B – False

C – Impossible to say

Answer

## Question 4

It is concluded from the passage that corporations rely on integrity and moral obligations as a way of demonstrating social responsibility.

A – True

B – False

C – Impossible to say

Answer

## Question 5

Supervisors have a duty to implement social responsibility within the corporation.

A – True

B – False

C – Impossible to say

Answer

## PASSAGE 2

There is a minimum right to paid holiday, but your employer may offer more than this. All employees are entitled to a minimum of 5.6 weeks paid leave per year. Employees who work for five days a week are entitled to 28 days per year annual leave. Employees who work part-time are entitled to the same level of holiday pro rata (5.6 times your normal working week) e.g. 16.8 days for someone working three days a week. All employees will start building up holiday entitlement as soon as they start work with the employer. The employer has the right to control when you take your holiday but you must get paid the same level of pay whilst on holiday. When you finish working for an employer you get paid for any holiday you have not taken. The employer may include bank and public holidays in your minimum entitlement. You continue to be entitled to your holiday leave throughout any additional maternity/paternity leave and adoption leave.

### Question 6

An employer is not allowed to offer you more than the minimum paid holiday.

A – True

B – False

C – Impossible to say

Answer [          ]

### Question 7

In addition to paternity leave you are entitled to your normal holiday.

A – True

B – False

C – Impossible to say

Answer [          ]

## Question 8

All employees only start building holiday leave 5.6 weeks after commencement of employment.

A – True

B – False

C – Impossible to say

Answer

## Question 9

Employees who receive more than the minimum holiday entitlement are often grateful to their employer.

A – True

B – False

C – Impossible to say

Answer

## Question 10

It is concluded from the passage, that your employer has no right to interfere when you choose to take your holiday leave.

A – True

B – False

C – Impossible to say

Answer

## PASSAGE 3

People pay National Insurance contributions in order to build up their entitlement to a state pension and other social security benefits. The amount that you pay is directly linked to the amount you earn. If you earn over a certain amount, your employer deducts Class 1 National Insurance contributions from your wages through the PAYE system. You pay a lower rate of National Insurance contributions if you're a member of your employer's 'contracted-out' pension scheme, or you're a married woman – or widow –who holds a valid 'election certificate'. Your employer also pays employer National Insurance contributions based on your earnings and on any benefits you get with your job, for example a company car. HMRC keeps track of your contributions through your National Insurance number. This is like an account number and is unique to you.

## Question 11

People pay National Insurance contributions in order to build up housing benefits.

A – True

B – False

C – Impossible to say

Answer

## Question 12

HMRC stands for 'Her Majesty's Revenue and Customs'.

A – True

B – False

C – Impossible to say

Answer

## Question 13

An employer pays National Insurance contributions if an employee has a company car.

A – True

B – False

C – Impossible to say

Answer [          ]

## Question 14

If you are a widow, you will pay more National Insurance contributions.

A – True

B – False

C – Impossible to say

Answer [          ]

## Question 15

If you are not earning money, you do not get taxed National Insurance.

A – True

B – False

C – Impossible to say

Answer [          ]

## PASSAGE 4

Franchises are very popular at the moment with an increasing number of people choosing to buy one, as opposed to starting out by setting up their own business. As a 'franchisee', you are buying a license to use the name, products, services, and management support systems of the 'franchiser' company. As a franchisee, the way you pay for the franchises may be through an initial fee, ongoing management fees, a share of your turnover, or a combination of all these depending on circumstances. A franchise business can take different legal forms – most are sole traders, partnerships or limited companies. The good news is that there is information to suggest that the franchise business sector is still growing. The vast majority of business franchisees in 2007 were in profit, a total of 93% compared to the 70% in 1991.

## Question 16

During 2007, the total number of business franchises that were not in profit totalled 7%.

A – True

B – False

C – Impossible to say

Answer

## Question 17

As the 'franchiser', you are buying a license to use the name, products and services of the franchised company.

A – True

B – False

C – Impossible to say

Answer

## Question 18

A franchise business can take different legal forms including Limited Liability Partnership (LLP).

A – True

B – False

C – Impossible to say

Answer [               ]

## Question 19

Franchising businesses were more popular in 1991 than in 2007.

A – True

B – False

C – Impossible to say

Answer [               ]

## Question 20

Franchising businesses will create more profits.

A – True

B – False

C – Impossible to say

Answer [               ]

# ANSWERS TO VERBAL REASONING TESTS – SUBSECTION 4

**Q1.** A, True

EXPLANATION = the passage clearly indicates that over the last few years, social responsibility to corporations has increased. For them to increase, it must mean that they have changed. Therefore this statement must be true.

**Q2.** A, True

EXPLANATION = the passage demonstrates different ways that social responsibility has influenced different aspects of our lives, and therefore makes this statement true.

**Q3.** C, Impossible to say

EXPLANATION = the passage does not mention anything about larger companies in relation to the Government, therefore it is impossible to say whether this is true or false.

**Q4.** A, True

EXPLANATION = the passage clearly demonstrates that ethics, integrity and morals are a way of maintaining social responsibility. Therefore this conclusion must be true.

**Q5.** C, Impossible to say

EXPLANATION = it is impossible to say whether supervisors have a duty to implement social responsibility in the workforce. The passage does not mention anything about supervisors in relation to social responsibilities, therefore you cannot make this conclusion.

**Q6.** B, False

EXPLANATION = an employer may offer more than the minimum paid holiday, therefore this statement must be false.

**Q7.** A, True

EXPLANATION = "you continue to be entitled to your holiday leave throughout any additional maternity/paternity leave", therefore this statement must be true.

**Q8.** B, False

EXPLANATION = the passage clearly indicates that you start building up holiday entitlement as "soon" as you start work, therefore this statement must be false.

**Q9.** C, Impossible to say

EXPLANATION = you cannot say based on the information you are provided with. The passage does not mention anything about employees being grateful for extra holiday entitlement, therefore you cannot form this conclusion.

**Q10.** B, False

EXPLANATION = the passage states your employer can control when you take your holiday leave, therefore this conclusion contradicts the information in the passage and so the conclusion must be false.

**Q11.** C, Impossible to say

EXPLANATION = although the passage makes reference to social security benefits, it does not confirm what type of benefits these are. You cannot say based on the information provided.

**Q12.** C, Impossible to say

EXPLANATION = the passage does not mention what the HMRC stands for. Although you may know this from prior knowledge to be fact, based on the information provided you are unable to draw this conclusion.

**Q13.** A, True

EXPLANATION = the passage states that "your employer also pays employer National Insurance contributions based on your earnings and on any benefits you get with your job, for example a company car". Therefore this conclusion must be true.

**Q14.** B, False

EXPLANATION = the passage clearly illustrates that widows pay 'a lower rate' of National Insurance contributions, therefore this conclusion is false.

**Q15.** C, Impossible to say

EXPLANATION = although you may know this to be true, the passage does not mention anything about people who are not earning money, therefore you cannot draw this conclusion.

**Q16.** A, True

EXPLANATION = the passage states that "the vast majority of business franchisees in 2007 were in profit, a total of 93%". Therefore, 7% of business franchises must have not been in profit, making the statement true.

**Q17.** B, False

EXPLANATION = the passage states that the 'franchisee' not the 'franchiser' is buying a license to use the name, products and other services. Therefore this statement must be false.

**Q18.** C, Impossible to say

EXPLANATION = we cannot assume Limited Liability Partnerships (LLP) is amongst the businesses that can take different legal forms. Therefore it is impossible to say whether this is true or false.

**Q19.** B, False

EXPLANATION = franchising businesses were more popular in 2007 than in 1991, therefore this contradicts the information in the passage and so the statement must be false.

**Q20.** C, Impossible to say

EXPLANATION = it is impossible to say whether franchising a business will definitely create more profits. Statistics of 2007 showed that 7% of companies did not make profits, so therefore not every company is going to make a profit.

# VERBAL REASONING TESTS

## (SUBSECTION 5)

# PASSAGE 1

In India, breast cancer has been on the increase, with an estimated 80,000 new cases diagnosed each year. Breast cancer increased approximately 50% between 1965 and 1985. This increase is said to be associated with improved lifestyles, longer life expectancies and greater urbanisation.

## Question 1

People who are living longer won't get breast cancer.

A – True

B – False

C – Impossible to say

Answer

## Question 2

India's breast cancer rate is much higher than other developed countries.

A – True

B – False

C – Impossible to say

Answer

## Question 3

If the number of breast cancer cases in 1965 was 3,500, the approximate number of breast cancer cases between 1965 and 1985 would be 5,250.

A – True

B – False

C – Impossible to say

Answer [                    ]

## Question 4

If new cases of cancer continued to be diagnosed at the estimated rate, after 3 years, there would be approximately 320,000 new cases of diagnosed people having breast cancer.

A – True

B – False

C – Impossible to say

Answer [                    ]

## Question 5

It can be concluded that the increase in life expectancy and greater urbanisation can be associated with breast cancer.

A – True

B – False

C – Impossible to say

Answer [                    ]

## PASSAGE 2

Janet and Steve have been married for twenty-seven years. They have a daughter called Jessica who is twenty-five. They all want to go on holiday together but cannot make up their minds where to go. Janet's first choice would be somewhere hot and sunny abroad. Her second choice would be somewhere in their home country that involves a sporting activity. She does not like hill-climbing or walking holidays but her third choice would be a skiing holiday. Steve's first choice would be a walking holiday in the hills somewhere in their home country and his second choice would be a sunny holiday abroad. He does not enjoy skiing. Jessica's first choice would be a skiing holiday and her second choice would be a sunny holiday abroad. Jessica's third choice would be a walking holiday in the hills of their home country.

### Question 6

Jessica's first choice would be a walking holiday in the hills of their home country.

A – True

B – False

C – Impossible to say

Answer 

### Question 7

Janet and Jessica have been married for twenty-seven years.

A – True

B – False

C – Impossible to say

Answer

## Question 8

Jessica would rather go skiing than go on a sunny holiday abroad.

A –True

B – False

C – Impossible to say

Answer

## Question 9

They decided to go on a walking holiday in their home country.

A – True

B – False

C – Impossible to say

Answer

## Question 10

All of their first choices were different.

A – True

B – False

C – Impossible to say

Answer

## PASSAGE 3

Technological change has had a huge impact on industries. These changes also effect software developments and service industries. Airlines, insurance companies and managerial positions often rely on new advances of technology. Over the years, it has become apparent that the future of technological changes are inevitable.

### Question 11

Technological change will effect only certain functions of an organisation, leaving other areas of the organisation free from technological change.

A – True

B – False

C – Impossible to say

Answer 

### Question 12

Technological change has already started.

A – True

B – False

C – Impossible to say

Answer

## Question 13

All companies rely on technological change.

A – True

B – False

C – Impossible to say

Answer

## Question 14

Airlines are one example that relies on the advances of new technology.

A – True

B – False

C – Impossible to say

Answer

## Question 15

The Government use these technological changes as a way of maintaining an effective and smooth-running society.

A – True

B – False

C – Impossible to say

Answer

## PASSAGE 4

Fire service employees who attain fifteen years' continuous service between 7th November 2003 and 30th June 2007 shall qualify for the long-service payment at the rate applicable at the time. Employees who are promoted in this time period will cease to qualify for the payment but will receive a minimum pay increase on promotion. When an employee on the retained duty system has not received a pay increase of at least 7% (for the same pattern and level of activity) following full implementation of the pay award effective from 7th November 2003, the fire and rescue authority may introduce arrangements to ensure that such an increase is achieved.

### Question 16

If an employee who is on the retained duty system has not received a pay increase of at least 7% following the introduction of the pay award, the fire and rescue service must introduce arrangements to ensure that such an increase is achieved.

A – True

B – False

C – Impossible to say

Answer

### Question 17

Employees who attain fifteen years' continuous service between 7th November 2003 and 30th June 2008 shall qualify for the long-service payment at the rate applicable at the time.

A – True

B – False

C – Impossible to say

Answer

## Question 18

The pay assimilation process on 7th November 2003 created a basic pay increase for all employees of more than 7%.

A – True

B – False

C – Impossible to say

Answer ☐

## Question 19

People who get promoted in the time period between 7th November 2003 and 30th June 2007 will still qualify for the long-service payment.

A – True

B – False

C – Impossible to say

Answer ☐

## Question 20

The authority of the fire and rescue service will ensure that people receive their payments which include their increase.

A – True

B – False

C – Impossible to say

Answer ☐

# ANSWERS TO VERBAL REASONING TESTS – SUBSECTION 5

**Q1.** C, Impossible to say

EXPLANATION = it is impossible to say whether people who are living longer will or will not get breast cancer, you cannot tell based on the information provided.

**Q2.** C, Impossible to say

EXPLANATION = you cannot tell whether India has a higher breast cancer rate compared to other developed countries. Therefore it is impossible to say.

**Q3.** A, True

EXPLANATION = 3,500 / 100 x 50 = 1750 + 3,500 = 5,250. This would be a 50% increase from 1965 to 1985, therefore the statement would be true.

**Q4.** B, False

EXPLANATION = after 3 years it would be 80,000 x 3 = 240,000. Therefore the statement must be false.

**Q5.** A, True

EXPLANATION = the passage clearly indicates that greater urbanisation and life expectancy can be associated with breast cancer, therefore the statement must be true.

**Q6.** B, False

EXPLANATION = Jessica's first choice would be a skiing holiday therefore it contradicts the passage and thus, must be false.

**Q7.** B, False

EXPLANATION = Janet and Steve have been married twenty-seven years, so therefore the statement must be false.

**Q8.** A, True

EXPLANATION = Jessica's first choice would be a skiing holiday. Her second choice would be a sunny holiday abroad. Therefore the statement must be true.

**Q9.** C, Impossible to say

EXPLANATION = the passage does not give any information on the decision they had come to in relation to where they would go on their holidays. Therefore you cannot make this conclusion.

**Q10.** A, True

EXPLANATION = Steve's first choice was a walking holiday. Jessica's first choice was a skiing holiday and Janet's first choice was somewhere hot and sunny abroad. Therefore the statement must be true.

**Q11.** C, Impossible to say

EXPLANATION = There is no evidence or information to suggest that certain areas of an organisation will not be affected from technological change.

**Q12.** A, True

EXPLANATION = the passage states that these changes have also effected software developments. This demonstrates that technological changes have already started, therefore this statement must be true.

**Q13.** C, Impossible to say

EXPLANATION = you cannot tell from the information provided whether all companies rely on technological changes, some may not. Therefore you cannot draw this conclusion.

**Q14.** A, True

EXPLANATION = the passage clearly illustrates airlines as being an example that relies on advanced technology. Therefore the statement must be true.

**Q15.** C, Impossible to say

EXPLANATION = the passage does not mention anything about the Government and how they use these technological changes. Therefore you cannot determine whether this statement is true or false.

**Q16.** B, False

EXPLANATION = this statement is false because the sentence states that the fire and rescue service 'may' introduce arrangements; it does not say they 'must'.

**Q17.** B, False

EXPLANATION = this statement is false because the sentence states 30th June 2008, instead of 30th June 2007 as stated in the passage.

**Q18.** C, Impossible to say

EXPLANATION = we cannot say that this statement is true or false. It makes no reference in the passage that 'all' employees receive a pay rise.

**Q19.** B, False

EXPLANATION = the passage clearly indicates that people who receive a promotion in this time period will cease to qualify for the long-service payment, therefore this statement is false.

**Q20.** A, True

EXPLANATION = the passage indicates that "the fire and rescue authority may introduce arrangements to ensure that such an increase is achieved". Therefore this statement must be true.

# CHAPTER 6

## *FAST STREAM E-TRAY TESTS*

The E-Tray exercise is also part of your assessment. This exercise will test your ability to handle workload which is typical of a Fast Streamer. The test is computer-based. You may have heard the term 'In-Tray' exercises. These tests are very similar in what they assess and how they are structured. The main difference between the two is that E-Tray is an online version, whereas In-Tray is paper-based. For the Civil Service Testing process, you will be taking the online version.

As we are unable to provide you with an exact account of an E-Tray exercise based on the fact it is computer-based, and this book is obviously paper-based, we have provided you with In-Tray style exercises that look and act similar to those of an E-Tray exercise. This will provide you with some knowledge and awareness of what to expect.

This test uses a series of emails and requests that arrive in an email inbox. The actual test is broken down into three sections:

# PART 1

## Reading and comprehending the background information.

- You will be presented with a lot of information in regards to a possible scenario you may encounter.
- This may include details about your 'job', the company you work for, details about colleagues and clients etc.
- All this information will need to be read carefully in order to work efficiently throughout the next two stages.
- This part of the exercise is not difficult, however, it is timed and the time limit is quite strict.
- Most candidates find it difficult to make use of the time effectively.
- Be sure to take notes, try to index the documents you are given, rather than copying them word for word.

# PART 2

## Identifying the least and most effective responses to a series of emails.

- You will be presented with emails, emails typical of the job you are applying for. Your job is to filter out the most important emails, answer them quickly and respond in the best way.
- Once you answer one email, you cannot return to it.
- The more emails you answer, will cause more emails to arrive in your inbox. The emails that arrive in your inbox are adapted to how you have answered the previous emails.
- Be sure to check all of the emails for attachments and important notifications.
- The background information you read in part 1 is fundamental. You need to have read that information thoroughly to proceed through the emails.
- These emails are designed to test how well you can organise yourself and your workload, how well you can prioritise and how well you can judge a situation, responding in the correct way.
- Pay attention to the smaller details. It is crucial that no information is overlooked.
- This part of the E-Tray test will decide whether you will make it to the Assessment Centre.

# PART 3

## Writing a response.

- This task requires you to write a response, usually in a form of a memo.
- This will test your ability to respond in a professional and effective way.
- The memo you write will relate to the information you acquired during stages 1 and 2.

## Writing style:

- Consider your writing style before attempting this task. You need to be able to structure an informative argument/response.
- It is generally considered that bullet pointing at this stage is not desirable.
- Remember to use paragraphs for every point you make, demonstrating a clear and concise structure.
- Try not to quote too much from the previous information. Instead, paraphrase that information, interpret it and analyse the situation.
- Try to remain objective whilst still remaining authoritative.
- Always look out for correct spelling, punctuation and grammar. Small details such as these are imperative!
- This part of the E-Tray will be evaluated and form part of your assessment mark if you make it through to the Assessment Centre.

## Overview of the practice E-Tray exercise

### Overview     ✕

The practice test has been provided with a clear intention to show you what you could expect when taking the E-Tray part of the Civil Service Fast Stream tests. The aim of this test is to allow you to engage with an email-based assessment and provide you with the experience of completing an E-Tray exercise.

E-Tray is a way of testing the candidate's ability to deal with workload in the form of emails. You will be asked to provide responses and make judgements about practical issues that you are likely to face in the Civil Service. These tests allow employers to assess how well a candidate can deal with prioritising, organising, responding and evaluating – all key attributes for becoming a civil servant.

This practice test will include a set of instructions, background information, and five email tasks. Although we have not provided you with a time limit, remember that in the real test you will have a time limit, so therefore we suggest that you practice at least one of these tasks under timed conditions.

## Instructions of the practice E-Tray exercise

### Task Instructions     ✕

The E-Tray exercise consists of three parts:

**1.** Review background information
**2.** Respond to emails
**3.** Written exercise

Task 1 is not assessed. You simply need to read through the background information carefully in order to gain an overview of the scenario.

Task 2 requires you to respond to a number of emails (in this case there will be 5). Each email will have multiple choice and you are to choose the most and least effective response.

Task 3 requires you to draft a sample response to deal with a request.

You will now be given some background information for your first exercise which you should read thoroughly and make notes. We have provided you with some space so you can write down your notes.

# E-TRAY PRACTICE

# PART 1 OF THE E-TRAY EXERCISE

# BACKGROUND INFORMATION

You have recently come back from holiday. There are 5 emails requiring your response.

Founded by co-directors Mark Ramsay and Tom Parks in 2002, Bedwell Consulting Partners has built up a valuable reputation specialising in small and local businesses. The firm began with the intention to ensure businesses have financial help and advice.

The Head Office, at which you work, is located in London. There are no other branches as of yet, but the manager is thinking of branching out.

The main areas that the company deals with in terms of consulting other businesses are:

- Management – strategic and operations
- Financial consultations
- Transfer skills and knowledge
- Projections and planning advice
- Performing quality control

The business is relatively new and is always looking for new clients. However the clientele base needs to follow certain levels of criteria:

- It must be UK-based
- Be a small businesses with no more than 30 employees
- Have an average annual income that doesn't exceed over £4 million

If clients do not meet one or more of these requirements, Bedwell Consulting Partners will not be able to work with them. Bedwell Consulting Partners want to ensure that maximum business potential can be made by taking clients only with the best possible success rate.

## YOUR ROLE

You have only been at Bedwell Consulting Partners for two weeks. You joined as a Team Leader, employed for your positive attitude, great knowledge, skill, key eye for detail and willingness to learn. Although the managing director, Tom Parks, tries to oversee day-to-day activities, he made it clear that he would be too busy to do this all of the time. Therefore you do have his support to make decisions without him when the situation requires.

Since being away, there have been some issues left unresolved and it is your duty to respond and deal with them. You must respond to the emails as soon as possible. You need to keep in mind that you will not be able to change, adapt or receive any further contact after your email is sent.

The date is: 12th November 2014

## BEDWELL CONSULTING PARTNERS CALENDER NOVEMBER 2014

| Sunday | Monday | Tuesday | Wednesday | Thursday | Friday | Saturday |
|---|---|---|---|---|---|---|
| | | | | | | 1 |
| 2 | 3 | 4 | 5 | 6 Meeting 9.00am | 7 | 8 |
| 9 | 10 | 11 | 12 | 13 | 14 | 15 |
| 16 | 17 Meeting 11.30am | 18 Training 9-12.30 | 19 | 20 | 21 | 22 |
| 23 | 24 | 25 | 26 | 27 | 28 Conference 10.00am | 29 |
| 30 | | | | | | |

WE ADVISE THAT YOU TAKE SOME NOTES BEFORE PROCEEDING TO
THE NEXT STAGE:

# PART 2 OF THE E-TRAY EXERCISE

## Email 1

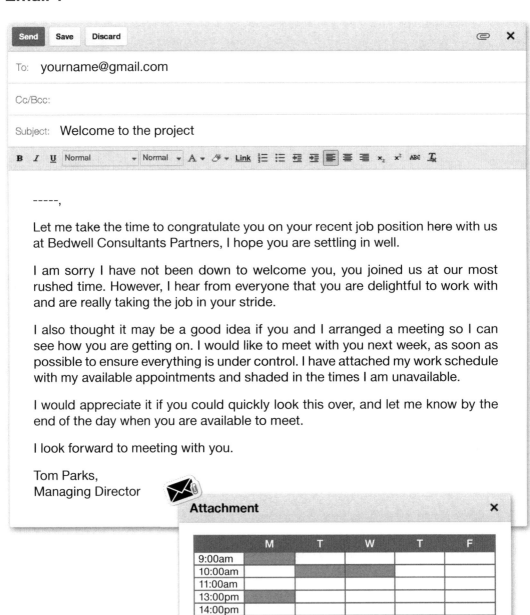

Send   Save   Discard

To: yourname@gmail.com

Cc/Bcc:

Subject: Welcome to the project

B  *I*  U  Normal  ▾  Normal ▾ A ▾ ✎ ▾ Link ☰ ☰ ☰ ☰ ☰ ☰ ☰ x₂ x² ABC

-----,

Let me take the time to congratulate you on your recent job position here with us at Bedwell Consultants Partners, I hope you are settling in well.

I am sorry I have not been down to welcome you, you joined us at our most rushed time. However, I hear from everyone that you are delightful to work with and are really taking the job in your stride.

I also thought it may be a good idea if you and I arranged a meeting so I can see how you are getting on. I would like to meet with you next week, as soon as possible to ensure everything is under control. I have attached my work schedule with my available appointments and shaded in the times I am unavailable.

I would appreciate it if you could quickly look this over, and let me know by the end of the day when you are available to meet.

I look forward to meeting with you.

Tom Parks,
Managing Director

**Attachment**                                                    ✕

|          | M | T | W | T | F |
|----------|---|---|---|---|---|
| 9:00am   | ▓ |   |   |   |   |
| 10:00am  |   | ▓ | ▓ |   |   |
| 11:00am  |   |   |   |   |   |
| 13:00pm  | ▓ |   |   |   |   |
| 14:00pm  |   |   |   |   |   |
| 15:00pm  |   |   |   | ▓ | ▓ |
| 16:00pm  |   |   |   |   |   |

*please note, Tuesday appointments are now unavailable*

## Responses:

| | Most Effective | Least Effective |
|---|---|---|
| Thank Mr Parks and let him know you will be available to meet anytime Thursday. | | |
| Do not reply. You are very busy and you are unsure of when you are going to be free. Turn up to Mr Parks' office when you have some free time and apologise for any inconvenience. | | |
| Thank Mr Parks for the welcome email and let him know you are available to meet with him Monday at 10.00am. | | |
| Thank Mr Parks for the welcome and let him know you are available to meet Wednesday at 10.00am | | |

## Email 2

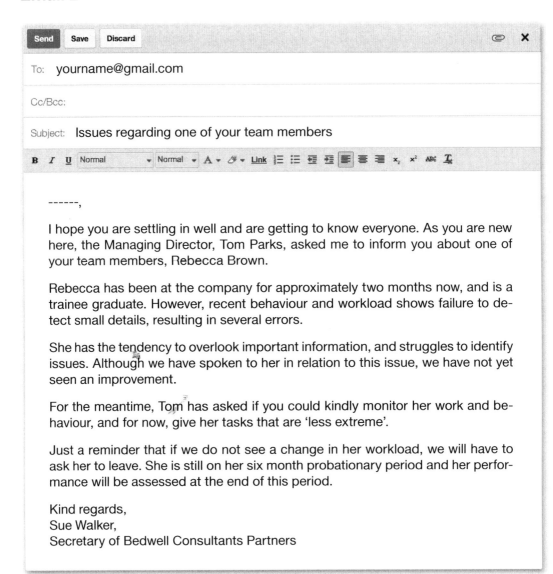

Send    Save    Discard

To:    yourname@gmail.com

Cc/Bcc:

Subject:    Issues regarding one of your team members

B  *I*  U  Normal  ▾  Normal ▾  A ▾  ✎ ▾  Link  ☰  ☷  ☶  ☵  ☰  ☰  ☰  x₂  x²  ABC  🖉

------,

I hope you are settling in well and are getting to know everyone. As you are new here, the Managing Director, Tom Parks, asked me to inform you about one of your team members, Rebecca Brown.

Rebecca has been at the company for approximately two months now, and is a trainee graduate. However, recent behaviour and workload shows failure to detect small details, resulting in several errors.

She has the tendency to overlook important information, and struggles to identify issues. Although we have spoken to her in relation to this issue, we have not yet seen an improvement.

For the meantime, Tom has asked if you could kindly monitor her work and behaviour, and for now, give her tasks that are 'less extreme'.

Just a reminder that if we do not see a change in her workload, we will have to ask her to leave. She is still on her six month probationary period and her performance will be assessed at the end of this period.

Kind regards,
Sue Walker,
Secretary of Bedwell Consultants Partners

## Responses:

| | Most Effective | Least Effective |
|---|---|---|
| Thank you for informing me. I will monitor her performance and give her a chance to prove herself. | | |
| Thank you for informing me Sue. | | |
| Thank you for informing me. I will be sure to give her only tasks that are less important. | | |
| Thank you, I will call her in for a meeting and discuss the issues you have presented. | | |

## Email 3

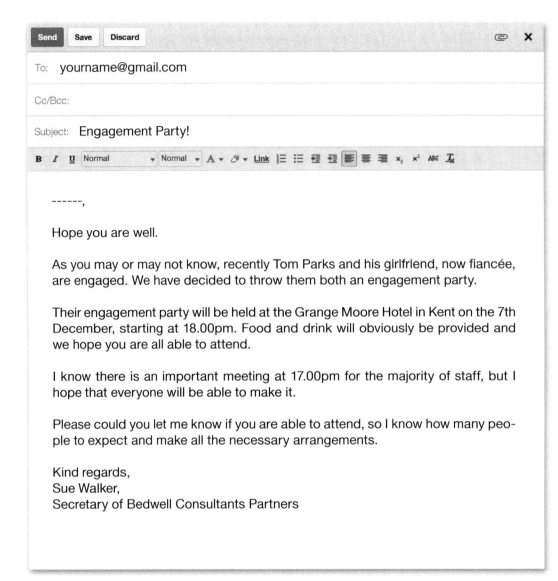

Send  Save  Discard

To: yourname@gmail.com

Cc/Bcc:

Subject: Engagement Party!

B  *I*  U  Normal  ▾ Normal ▾  A ▾  ✎ ▾  Link  ≔  ≔  ⇥  ⇥  ≣  ≣  ≣  x₂  x²  ABC  ℐ

------,

Hope you are well.

As you may or may not know, recently Tom Parks and his girlfriend, now fiancée, are engaged. We have decided to throw them both an engagement party.

Their engagement party will be held at the Grange Moore Hotel in Kent on the 7th December, starting at 18.00pm. Food and drink will obviously be provided and we hope you are all able to attend.

I know there is an important meeting at 17.00pm for the majority of staff, but I hope that everyone will be able to make it.

Please could you let me know if you are able to attend, so I know how many people to expect and make all the necessary arrangements.

Kind regards,
Sue Walker,
Secretary of Bedwell Consultants Partners

## Responses:

| | Most Effective | Least Effective |
|---|---|---|
| Thank you for letting me know Sue, I am able to attend the party, and I'm looking forward to it. | | |
| Do not reply. | | |
| Thank you for letting me know Sue. | | |
| Thank you for the email Sue. However, I feel slightly disheartened that I am the last person to know about their engagement. | | |

## Email 4

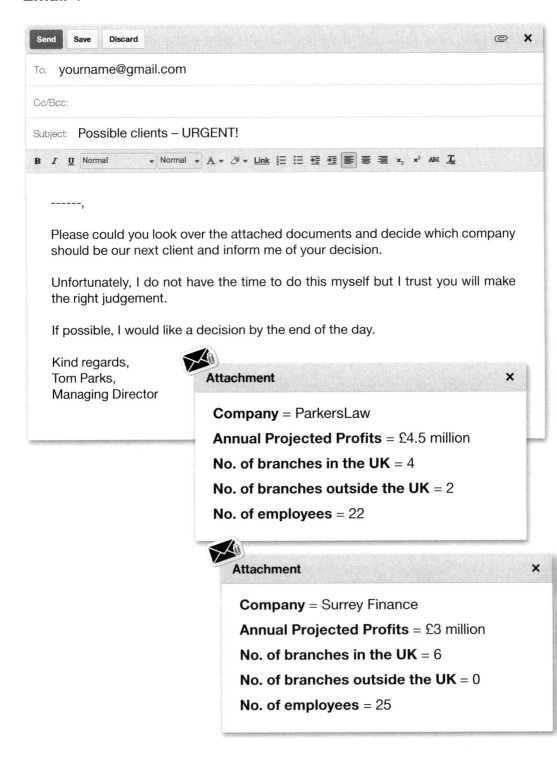

**Send**  Save  Discard

To: yourname@gmail.com

Cc/Bcc:

Subject: Possible clients – URGENT!

B  *I*  U  Normal  ▾ | Normal ▾ | A ▾ ✎ ▾ Link ...

------,

Please could you look over the attached documents and decide which company should be our next client and inform me of your decision.

Unfortunately, I do not have the time to do this myself but I trust you will make the right judgement.

If possible, I would like a decision by the end of the day.

Kind regards,
Tom Parks,
Managing Director

**Attachment**                                    ✕

**Company** = ParkersLaw

**Annual Projected Profits** = £4.5 million

**No. of branches in the UK** = 4

**No. of branches outside the UK** = 2

**No. of employees** = 22

**Attachment**                                    ✕

**Company** = Surrey Finance

**Annual Projected Profits** = £3 million

**No. of branches in the UK** = 6

**No. of branches outside the UK** = 0

**No. of employees** = 25

**Attachment** ✕

**Company** = British Gas

**Annual Projected Profits** = £8 million

**No. of branches in the UK** = 120

**No. of branches outside the UK** = 118

**No. of employees** = 512

## Responses:

|  | Most Effective | Least Effective |
|---|---|---|
| After analysing each company, I believe our next client should be ParkersLaw. | | |
| After analysing each company, I believe our next client should be Surrey Finance. | | |
| After analysing each company, I believe our next client should be British Gas. | | |
| After analysing each company, I don't think any of the companies match up to our requirements. | | |

## Email 5

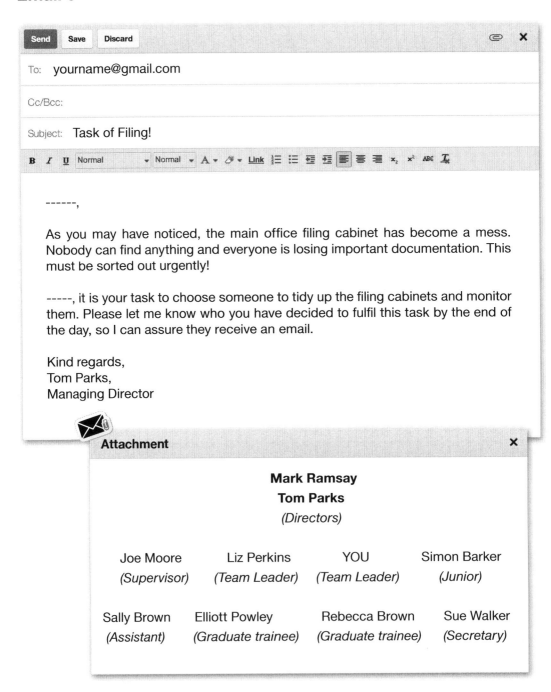

Send  Save  Discard

To: yourname@gmail.com

Cc/Bcc:

Subject: Task of Filing!

B  *I*  U  Normal  ▾ Normal ▾ A ▾ ◇ ▾ Link ≔ ≔ ≖ ≖ ▤ ▤ ▤ x₂ x² ABC I

------,

As you may have noticed, the main office filing cabinet has become a mess. Nobody can find anything and everyone is losing important documentation. This must be sorted out urgently!

-----, it is your task to choose someone to tidy up the filing cabinets and monitor them. Please let me know who you have decided to fulfil this task by the end of the day, so I can assure they receive an email.

Kind regards,
Tom Parks,
Managing Director

**Attachment**

**Mark Ramsay**
**Tom Parks**
*(Directors)*

| Joe Moore | Liz Perkins | YOU | Simon Barker |
|---|---|---|---|
| *(Supervisor)* | *(Team Leader)* | *(Team Leader)* | *(Junior)* |

| Sally Brown | Elliott Powley | Rebecca Brown | Sue Walker |
|---|---|---|---|
| *(Assistant)* | *(Graduate trainee)* | *(Graduate trainee)* | *(Secretary)* |

**Responses:**

|  | Most Effective | Least Effective |
|---|---|---|
| I have decided to give the filing job to Joe. | | |
| I have decided to do the filing job myself. | | |
| I have decided to give Simon the task of filing. | | |
| I have decided to give the task to Liz. | | |

# PART 3 OF THE E-TRAY EXERCISE

## Written Exercise

A possible client is unsure about the services Bedwell Consulting Partners has to offer. The client is called Randall Financing, and is a small company of 20 employees.

Write a letter to send to Randall Financing highlighting the key areas and subject expertise, reinforcing the requirements needed and issuing a standard introduction of who Bedwell Consulting Partners are, what they do and what they offer.

DRAFTS / NOTES

**Response:**

TO: --------

From: -----------

Date:

Subject:

# ANSWERS TO E-TRAY PRACTICE

## Email 1

Thank Mr Parks for the welcome email and let him know you are available to meet with him Monday at 10.00am.

- *This would be the **MOST EFFECTIVE** response as it's the soonest availability for a meeting.*

Thank Mr Parks for the welcome and let him know you are available to meet Wednesday at 10.00am

- *This would be the **LEAST EFFECTIVE** response. It's the least effective because it clashes with another appointment.*

Thank Mr Parks and let him know you will be available to meet anytime Thursday.

- *This would be an ineffective response because they ask for the soonest available time, this would not be it.*

Do not reply. You are very busy and you are unsure of when you are going to be free. Turn up to Mr Parks' office when you have some free time and apologise for any inconvenience.

- *This would be ineffective because not replying is inconsiderate and shows lack of professionalism.*

## Email 2

Thank you for informing me. I will monitor her performance and give her a chance to prove herself.

- *This would be the **MOST EFFECTIVE** response as it allows you to analyse the issues yourself and not jump to any conclusions too soon.*

Thank you for informing me. I will be sure to give her only tasks that are less important.

- *This would be the **LEAST EFFECTIVE** response, it will not allow the employee to improve her performance and therefore would not be addressing the situation.*

Thank you for informing me Sue.

- *This would be an 'ok' response as it allows Sue to know you received her email and you have taken in the information.*

Thank you, I will call her in for a meeting and discuss the issues you have presented.

- *This would not be an appropriate response because you are new to your role and therefore you have not yet seen her performance for yourself.*


## Email 3

Thank you for letting me know Sue, I am able to attend the party, and I'm looking forward to it.

- *This is the **MOST EFFECTIVE** response as it informs Sue that you are able to attend and you received the email.*

Thank you for the email Sue. However, I feel slightly disheartened that I am the last person to know about their engagement.

- *This is the **LEAST EFFECTIVE** response because it is unprofessional and the incorrect way to handle a situation.*

Do not reply.

- *This response does not let Sue know whether you are able to attend or if you received the email.*

Thank you for letting me know Sue.

- *This is an 'ok' response because it makes Sue aware that you have received her email.*


## Email 4

After analysing each company, I believe our next client should be Surrey Finance.

- *This is the **MOST EFFECTIVE** response because it meets all the* *requirements of the company. (Remember to look at the background information given in stage 1).*

After analysing each company, I believe our next client should be British Gas.

- *This would be the **LEAST EFFECTIVE** response because its projected annual income is considerably higher to what the company looks for in clients, there are more employees and branches outside the UK, all of which are not suitable.*

After analysing each company, I believe our next client should be ParkersLaw.

- *This is an ineffective response because it earns more money than suitable to be a client for the company.*

After analysing each company, I don't think any of the companies match up to our requirements.

- *This is not an appropriate response because at least one of them does match up with the company requirements.*


## Email 5

I have decided to give Simon the task of filing.

- *This would be the **MOST EFFECTIVE** response because Simon is a junior, and filing would be a typical task for that job.*

I have decided to give the filing job to Joe.

- *This would be the **LEAST EFFECTIVE** response because Joe is a supervisor and therefore has other, more important responsibilities.*

I have decided to do the filing job myself.

- *This would be an ineffective response because you should be leading a team of people, rather than doing work that could be given to someone else.*

I have decided to give the task to Liz.

- *This would be an ineffective response because Liz is also a Team Leader and therefore could give the task to somebody else.*

## Written Exercise

(Here is a sample answer which would be an adequate and professional response).

TO: --------

From: -----------

Date: 12th November 2014

Subject: Enquires regarding Bedwell Consulting Partners

Thank you for your recent enquires. We have taken it upon ourselves to research Randall Financing in order to provide you with accurate information.

Let me start off by saying a little about our company. Here at Bedwell Consulting Partners **we offer expertise and long-term help and advice to consult businesses and help them fully reach their business potential.**

Founded in 2002, we have continuously grown as a consulting business and **gained a valuable reputation** within the industry. Our company aims to **provide local and small businesses in areas such as management, financing, skills, knowledge, projection planning and performing quality control to ensure companies are fully equipped and ready to succeed.**

In order to become a client of ours, your business has to meet some requirements. **We take clients who are only based in the UK.** We are hoping to branch out soon, but for the meantime we do not have the equipment or necessities needed to support clients outside of the United Kingdom.

Secondly, **businesses have to be small-scale.** We only take clients with no **more than 30 employees,** and from your recent enquiry, you certainly meet this requirement.

We also only take clients **whose projection annual income is less than £4 million.** This is to ensure that we remain effective and relevant to your business needs.

Unfortunately, **if you do not meet anyone of these requirements we are unable to work with you.** However, if you do meet the requirements to become part of our clientele base, **please feel free to send us an email if you require more information,** or you have decided to work alongside us.

We look forward to hearing from you here at Bedwell Consulting Partners,

Kind Regards,

------

- This sample email addresses the main points in relation to what the business does and what it has to offer.

- The email describes all the important and relevant information which potential clients would want to know i.e. are they eligible clients for the business, do they meet the criteria etc.

- The email interacts with the client by offering more interaction and communication.

- The email is well versed, grammatically correct, good punctuation and formally written.

# E-TRAY - TEST 1

# PART 1 OF THE E-TRAY EXERCISE

# BACKGROUND INFORMATION

The Department of Health (DH) under Government maintenance has implemented a new policy.

The 'Dementia Challenge' was launched in 2012 by the Prime Minister David Cameron. The PM describes dementia as being one of many issues that 'we' as a society face as the population ages.

The programme is designed to ensure a difference in the lives of so many people dealing with dementia. This programme doesn't only look after the person who suffers with dementia, but offers a whole support system to family and friends. This programme is linked to the National Dementia Strategy whereby it creates quality services to tackle and deal with dementia.

Under the programme, it implemented three groups which all focus on different areas of dementia and help provide new strategies and support systems:

- Creating 'dementia friendly' communities
- Health and social care
- Improving research on dementia

Since the start-up of the programme, reports have been published in order to demonstrate how the programme has progressed. However, such research is still looking for new ideas and different ways to tackle the issues surrounding dementia and how 'we' can create more of an awareness.

The initial targeted audience for this programme was mainly aimed at health professionals to help provide major improvements in dementia care and research.

## AIMS AND OBJECTIVES

The Government have set aims and objectives for the Dementia Challenge programme. These aims and objectives include:

- Creating dementia-friendly communities.
- Create more awareness for businesses.
- An innovation challenge prize is to be rewarded.
- Addressing the needs and support of people living with dementia.
- Making improvements in health and care.
- Improving research standards and ensure maximum potential can be made with more Government funds.

## RESEARCH

The word dementia describes a range of symptoms that occur when the brain is damaged by diseases. This may include Alzheimer's or a series of strokes. Around 670,000 in England live with dementia. A number which is said to double in the next 30 years if a cure is not found.

Dementia symptoms include loss of memory, difficulty thinking and can affect language ability. Dementia affects people in different ways and progression of symptoms will vary.

There are different types of dementia such as:

- **Vascular dementia** – blood and oxygen vessels become blocked resulting in lack of oxygen entering the brain. This type of dementia can form suddenly or gradually get worse. Many people experience difficulty with problem solving, thinking, concentrating and confusion.

- **Mixed dementia** – this is when someone suffers more than one type of dementia. They have a mixture of symptoms.

- **Alzheimer's** – brain cells are surrounded by abnormal proteins and the internal structures become damaged. Chemical connections become lost and brain cells die. Symptoms include day-to-day memory loss, difficulty finding the right words, struggling to make decisions and confused states of mind.

- **Frontotemporal dementia** – the front and side parts of the brain become damaged. Symptoms include severe changes in personality, behaviour and speech.

These types of dementia occur at different stages and progress at different times. As dementia progresses, more help is needed. Dementia suffers may find themselves unable to perform tasks they usually do, or they may find it difficult to say what they think.

The majority of cases cannot be cured. Despite research trying to find some solution to help improve cases of dementia, it will be a long time until one is found. Thus, people with dementia must be assured of the best advice, information and support to ensure they are fully aware of the disease and are provided with the right care and support that is required.

The Government have recently launched a television advert showing the effects of living with dementia in order to build awareness.

# POSSIBLE WAYS TO IMPROVE DEMENTIA CARE AWARENESS

- The Government plan to set up an innovation challenge for transforming the care of dementia. The challenge gives a £1 million prize to NHS staff if they can come up with an innovated idea for offering ways of better quality of care.

- Support from businesses on the challenge of dementia. Businesses will try and play a more active role in creating a more 'friendly' environment towards dementia.

- Doubling the funding for research by 2015 to £66 million. The research funds will increase from £26 million from 2009/2010 to approximately £66 million by 2015.

# YOUR TEAM

**Linda Andrews** – Chairman of the group committee at the Department of Health. Linda is responsible for ensuring everyone is on board with the task in hand and to ensure everyone knows what their duties are. Any issues, questions or queries should be reported to her co-chairman David Brown, who will act as a facilitator between all of the people working on this programme and herself.

**David Brown** – Co-chairman of the dementia challenge programme. He acts as Linda's assistant who will generate feedback and facilitate information between Linda and the rest of the team. His duty is to follow Linda's instructions and make sure the team are working efficiently and ensure maximum work ethic.

**Billy Crayford** – Billy is in charge of all financial data. Before a proposition can be implemented or a new idea enforced, Billy needs to check the funds and all the financial implications regarding that idea or proposition. All ideas should be financially checked once you have approval from Linda.

# YOUR ROLE

You are a graduate trainee who has just joined the programme. You are new to the programme and do not have that much experience or knowledge in the matter.

You were employed for your creativity and attention to detail. You like to put your ideas across and you always show willingness to participate.

The task for the group working on the dementia challenge programme is to come up with a new, innovative idea that can help improve one of the areas of dementia. These include **creating dementia-friendly communities, health and social care and improving dementia research.** You are also in charge of responding to emails, telephone calls and other queries concerning the project. You are to report to Linda only with important and serious issues.

The Prime Minister has set a fund of £5 million for a good, innovative idea. Your task is to implement the new strategy within the next six months.

WE ADVISE THAT YOU TAKE SOME NOTES BEFORE PROCEEDING TO THE NEXT STAGE:

# PART 2 OF THE E-TRAY EXERCISE - TEST 1

## Email 1

Send    Save    Discard

To:  yourname@gmail.com

Cc/Bcc:

Subject:  Dealing with the press

B  *I*  U  Normal    ▾  Normal  ▾  A ▾  ✎ ▾  Link  ≣ ≣ ⧉ ⧉ ▋ ≣ ≣  x₂  x²  ᴬᴮᶜ  𝐓ₓ

-----,

You may be aware that in the last week or so, some of our information regarding a proposed innovative prize of £1 million to NHS staff was revealed.

The press are all over the information, and calling the Government project a "stunt: a way of fixing a problem we created in the first place". We need to address this issue as a matter of urgency.

I know you are new to the project, but you were picked for your creative thinking and attention to detail. I would like you to file a press release regarding this issue. Trust your instincts and make the best judgement you see fit.

Kind regards,
David Brown

## Responses:

| | Most Effective | Least Effective |
|---|---|---|
| Indicate in your press release that this is a false rumour and that the Government are not implementing any strategies or incentives regarding a £1 million prize for NHS staff. Ensure the Government are trying to come up with new ideas to tackle dementia, but unfortunately this isn't one of them. | | |
| Ensure the press that the Government are coming up with different ways of tackling new and different incentives regarding the care of dementia, but state that no final decision has been made as of yet. | | |
| Use the press release to initiate the £1 million prize for NHS staff. State the incentive behind it and generate all the details regarding the prize to prompt a response from the press. Using the press will generate a 'buzz' for your upcoming project idea. | | |
| Tell the press that you have no information to disclose as of yet and file a complaint against the press for disclosing information regarding private Government matters. | | |

## Email 2

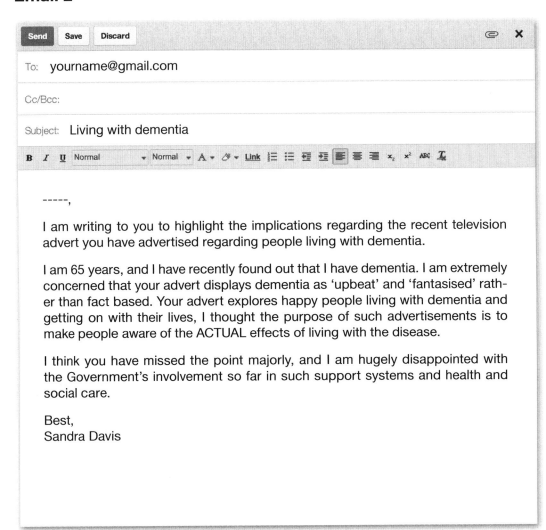

-----,

I am writing to you to highlight the implications regarding the recent television advert you have advertised regarding people living with dementia.

I am 65 years, and I have recently found out that I have dementia. I am extremely concerned that your advert displays dementia as 'upbeat' and 'fantasised' rather than fact based. Your advert explores happy people living with dementia and getting on with their lives, I thought the purpose of such advertisements is to make people aware of the ACTUAL effects of living with the disease.

I think you have missed the point majorly, and I am hugely disappointed with the Government's involvement so far in such support systems and health and social care.

Best,
Sandra Davis

## Responses:

| | Most Effective | Least Effective |
|---|---|---|
| Apologise to Sandra and state what the advert was supposed to do, and that you were sorry for any misconceptions the advert may contain. Demonstrate what the Government is trying to achieve and explain that the Government are working on enforcing new incentives and strategies. | | |
| Tell Sandra that she may have overlooked the advert and the point it was trying to make. Explain that the Government's ideas are 100% focused on portraying the life of people living with dementia and that they succeed getting their views across. | | |
| Do not reply. It will only upset Sandra more and could cause a bigger issue than necessary. | | |
| Inform Linda of these negative comments and ask how to proceed. She will want to deal with this problem directly to ensure the issue is dealt with correctly. | | |

## Email 3

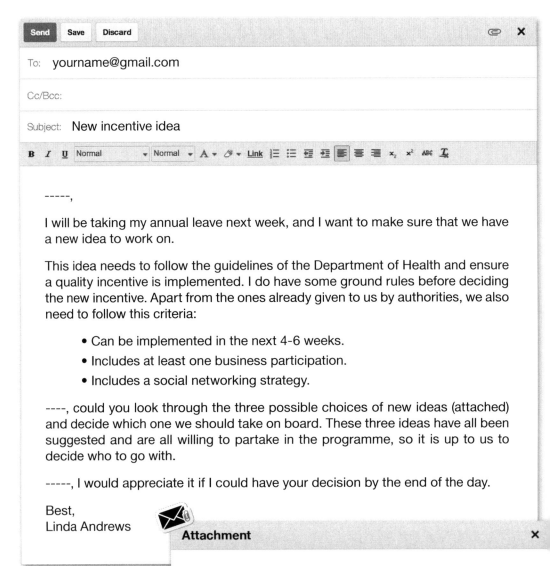

Send    Save    Discard

To:   yourname@gmail.com

Cc/Bcc:

Subject:   **New incentive idea**

**B** *I* <u>U</u>   Normal    Normal   A ▾   ✎ ▾   Link   ...

-----,

I will be taking my annual leave next week, and I want to make sure that we have a new idea to work on.

This idea needs to follow the guidelines of the Department of Health and ensure a quality incentive is implemented. I do have some ground rules before deciding the new incentive. Apart from the ones already given to us by authorities, we also need to follow this criteria:

- Can be implemented in the next 4-6 weeks.
- Includes at least one business participation.
- Includes a social networking strategy.

----, could you look through the three possible choices of new ideas (attached) and decide which one we should take on board. These three ideas have all been suggested and are all willing to partake in the programme, so it is up to us to decide who to go with.

-----, I would appreciate it if I could have your decision by the end of the day.

Best,
Linda Andrews

**Attachment**    ✕

**Company** = National Bank Association

**Projected funds for project** = £3 million

**How long it will take to implement** = 16 weeks

**Idea** = create a TV documentary exploring the lives of people with dementia. Create awareness about the symptoms, what it's like to care for someone suffering with dementia, how they overcome the disease (in terms of mentally dealing with it)

**Attachment**                                              ✕

**Company** = Retail companies (including New Look and Topshop)

**Projected funds for project** = £1.5million

**How long it will take to implement** = 3 weeks

**Idea** = launch a fashion show with a 'catwalk' with models that have all suffered with dementia. Sale tickets and raise an awareness whilst having fun and learning about the importance of dementia.

**Attachment**                                              ✕

**Company** = Rydell Secondary School

**Projected funds for project** = N/A

**How long it will take to implement** = 6 weeks

**Idea** = get children from the school to create flyers and posters and other forms of advertising to be displayed throughout the county. They will work on the designs and sketches themselves and then they can be professionally created into ways of advertisements.

## Responses:

|  | Most Effective | Least Effective |
|---|---|---|
| I have decided that the next idea we should work on is for the National Bank Association. |  |  |
| I have decided that the next idea we should work on is for the retail companies. |  |  |
| I have decided that that the next we should work on is for the Rydell Secondary School. |  |  |
| I have decided that none of these ideas are suitable for our next project |  |  |

## Email 4

-----,

Attached in the email is a calendar for the next six weeks with all the dates that are important launches for advertising strategies.

Our new idea of the retail company fashion show needs to be held in the next 4-6 weeks.

Please note there are some things to consider:

- The fashion show needs to come after the social networking launch date.
- The fashion show needs to be launched 1 week after the press conference.
- The fashion show needs to be the day before the photo-shoot.
- The fashion show needs to be 8 days before the meeting with health magazines.

Please can you schedule in the date that the retail company fashion show will take place.

Thank you,
David Brown

**Attachment** ✕

# November 2014

| Sunday | Monday | Tuesday | Wednesday | Thursday | Friday | Saturday |
|--------|--------|---------|-----------|----------|--------|----------|
|  |  |  |  |  |  | 1 |
| 2 | 3 | 4 | 5 | 6 | 7 | 8 |
| 9 | 10 | 11 | 12 | 13 | 14 | 15 |
| 16 | 17 | 18 | 19 | 20 | 21 Social networking launch | 22 |
| 23 | 24 Press Conference | 25 | 26 | 27 | 28 | 29 |
| 30 |  |  |  |  |  |  |

# December 2014

| Sunday | Monday | Tuesday | Wednesday | Thursday | Friday | Saturday |
|--------|--------|---------|-----------|----------|--------|----------|
|  | 1 | 2 Photo-shoot | 3 | 4 | 5 | 6 |
| 7 | 8 | 9 Meeting with health magazine | 10 | 11 | 12 | 13 |
| 14 | 15 | 16 | 17 | 18 | 19 | 20 |
| 21 | 22 | 23 | 24 | 25 | 26 | 27 |
| 28 | 29 | 30 | 31 |  |  |  |

## Responses:

| | Most Effective | Least Effective |
|---|---|---|
| The scheduled date for the fashion show will be the 9th December 2014. | | |
| The scheduled date for the fashion show will be the 27th November 2014. | | |
| The scheduled date for the fashion show will be the 1st December 2014. | | |

## Email 5

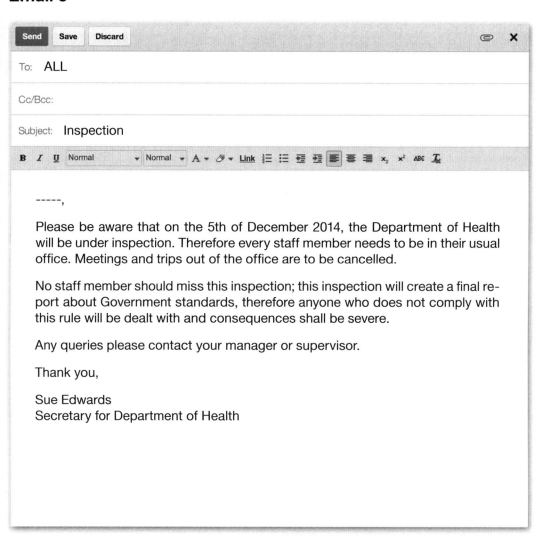

-----,

Please be aware that on the 5th of December 2014, the Department of Health will be under inspection. Therefore every staff member needs to be in their usual office. Meetings and trips out of the office are to be cancelled.

No staff member should miss this inspection; this inspection will create a final report about Government standards, therefore anyone who does not comply with this rule will be dealt with and consequences shall be severe.

Any queries please contact your manager or supervisor.

Thank you,

Sue Edwards
Secretary for Department of Health

## Responses:

| | Most Effective | Least Effective |
|---|---|---|
| Thank you for letting me know David. | | |
| Thank you for letting me know David. However, could you tell me how long approximately the inspection will take so I don't schedule any meetings during that time? Thank you. | | |
| No response is required for this email. | | |
| Thank you for letting me know. However, I have already arranged an important meeting, so I won't be able to make the inspection. | | |

# PART 3 OF E-TRAY EXERCISE – TEST 1

## Written Exercise

You are working on brainstorms regarding a new and innovative project to promote dementia and create more awareness about the disease. Your task is to draft an email to the chairman of the Dementia Challenge programme suggesting your idea.  You do not have to include any financial information, but using the information you have previously been given, come up with one example of an idea of an advertising strategy, the reasons for your choice, how it will benefit the Government and unique information that you think makes your idea stand out.

DRAFTS / NOTES

**Response:**

TO: --------

From: -----------

Date:

Subject:

# ANSWERS TO E-TRAY EXERCISE – TEST 1

## Email 1

Ensure the press that the Government are coming up with different ways of tackling new and different incentives regarding the care of dementia, but state that no final decision has been made as of yet.

- *This would be the **MOST EFFECTIVE** response. It deals with the press in a professional manner. Although you are not disclosing any information, you have not disregarded any rumours or agreed to them. You will be able to deal with this rumour when the time comes and when a decision has finally been made.*

Use the press release to initiate the £1 million prize for NHS staff. State the incentive behind it and generate all the details regarding the prize to prompt a response from the press. Using the press will generate a 'buzz' for your upcoming project idea.

- *This would be the **LEAST EFFECTIVE** response. You do not have the authority to issue a press release that affects the Government plans in the future. This idea has not been set in stone and is still being debated, therefore advertising the programme incentive is unprofessional and unproductive.*

Indicate in your press release that this is a false rumour and that the Government are not implementing any strategies or incentives regarding a £1 million prize for NHS staff. Ensure the Government are trying to come up with new ideas to tackle dementia, but unfortunately this isn't one of.

- *Giving the press false information could affect your incentive in the long run. This would not be a good solution because the people in society may find it hard to trust your incentive if you have already lied about it before. Therefore you should avoid ruling out the idea and telling the press it is false, when it may possibly be true.*

Tell the press that you have no information to disclose as of yet and file a complaint against the press for disclosing information regarding private Government matters.

- *Filing a complaint about the press when the incentive may be true in the long run, could affect the reputation of the project. Filing a complaint will only stir up more unwanted attention and draw away from the bigger picture which is the dementia challenge programme.*

## Email 2

Apologise to Sandra and state what the advert was supposed to do, and that you were sorry for any misconceptions the advert may contain. Demonstrate what the Government is trying to achieve and explain that the Government are working on enforcing new incentives and strategies.

- *This response would be the **MOST EFFECTIVE**. It deals with the issue in a sensitive and professional manner and allows Sandra to feel as though her thoughts have been heard and considered.*

Tell Sandra that she may have overlooked the advert and the point it was trying to make. Explain that the Government's ideas are 100% focused on portraying the life of people living with dementia and that they succeed getting their views across.

- *This would be the **LEAST EFFECTIVE** response. This will consequently make the situation worse and therefore could cause more problems in the future. You need to be able to show you can deal with such issues in a sensitive way.*

Do not reply. It will only upset Sandra more and could cause a bigger issue than necessary.

- *This is not effective. Not replying to Sandra shows lack of professionalism and does not deal with the issue directly. The Government need to demonstrate quality service and professionalism.*

Inform Linda of this negative comments and ask how to proceed. She will want to deal with this problem directly to ensure the issue is dealt with correctly.

- *This would not be necessary. You are in charge of responding to emails. Taking it to Linda shows your lack of ability to deal with such issues, issues that you should be able to tackle. Linda only needs to be informed if the situation was serious and vitally important.*

## Email 3

I have decided that the next idea we should work on is for the retail companies.

- This would be the **MOST EFFECTIVE** response. It fits in with the Government *funds of £5 million. It follows all the criteria that Linda set out in the email, and would be a mass advertising strategy to get involved with dementia.*

I have decided that the next idea we should work on is for the National Bank Association.

- This *would be the* **LEAST EFFECTIVE** *response. The project needs to be implemented in a matter of 4-6 weeks, this project takes 16 weeks to complete, therefore does not follow the criteria set out for the project.*

I have decided that that the next we should work on is for the Rydell Secondary School.

- This *response does not give you any indication as to the funds needed for the project. Also, compared to the retail company project, this is slightly small-scale and* won't generate a huge awareness.

I have decided that none of these ideas are suitable for our next project.

- *This response is wrong because one of these ideas would be a suitable one.*


## Email 4

The scheduled date for the fashion show will be the 1st December 2014.

- *This would be the* **MOST EFFECTIVE** *response because it corresponds with all the information in the email and fits in with the criteria of when it needs to be launched in accordance to everything else.*

The scheduled date for the fashion show will be the 9th December 2014.

- *This would be the* **LEAST EFFECTIVE** *because it clashes with the meeting with the health magazine.*

The scheduled date for the fashion show will be the 27th November 2014.

- *This response would be irrelevant because it does not meet all the necessary requirements in regards to when the fashion show should be in accordance to when everything else is launched.*

## Email 5

No response is required for this email.

- *This would be the **MOST EFFECTIVE** response. If you notice, the email was sent to all employees therefore it does not require a direct response.*

Thank you for letting me know. However, I have already arranged an important meeting, so I won't be able to make the inspection.

- *This would be the **LEAST EFFECTIVE** response. The email clearly states that under no exception shall employees miss the inspection. Therefore this email would be unprofessional and shows the inability to comply with rules and regulations.*

Thank you for letting me know David.

- *This would be an 'ok' response, but is not really necessary. The email was sent to everyone, therefore does not necessarily require a response from staff.*

Thank you for letting me know David. However, could you tell me how long approximately the inspection will take so I don't schedule any meetings during that time? Thank you.

- *This is also an 'ok' response but again, it's not necessary. The email was written by the secretary of the Department of Health and states that any queries to speak to your manager, therefore this would be an inappropriate response.*

## Written Exercise

For this response there is no right or wrong idea. You could have chosen any idea to promote the dementia challenge programme. The main aim of this task is to ensure that you provide relevant information regarding your idea and how this could benefit the Governments strategy at promoting awareness for people living with dementia. Some ideas that you could have come up:

- *Social networking campaign, TV campaign, Fashion show, Documentary style short-film, Print based / online based campaign*

Make sure that your email is grammatically correct, you have used the right punctuation and your spelling is correct. Remember this email is being addressed to the Chairman of the group committee for this project, so structure your email professionally and formally.

(Here is an example of the type of email you could have written).

---

TO: Linda Andrews
From: -----------
Date: 14th November 2014
Subject: New idea for advertising strategy

Linda,

My idea for the new advertising strategy is a fashion show with a documentary element. Dementia is always conveyed in a negative and upsetting way, and I believe that we could attract more attention and gain more awareness if we put a slight twist on this.

Using a fashion show, we would promote dementia from a first person point of view. We will use models who have all experienced dementia and therefore this adds a personal and experienced element to the campaign.

Throughout the fashion show, we can break it up into parts, whereby in each 'break' we play a short documentary of one of the models. This documentary will include their experiences with living with dementia. Not only does this create a sense of realism, but will also create some educational purpose in regards to what life is really like living with dementia.

Businesses such as New Look, Topshop, H&M and River Island etc. are all welcome to sponsor the clothes for the fashion show. Not only will this create style and elegance for the show, but will allow the Government to branch into the business world, and implement advertising strategies throughout the use of their companies.

Fashion shows are becoming increasingly popular and can be aimed at all ages and all types of people. I believe this creative idea will not only engage a variety of people, but can be created to attract a mass audience, therefore creating mass awareness.

I look forward to your feedback,

Kind regards,

-----

- Addresses your idea clearly and effectively using the correct grammar, spelling and punctuation.

- Demonstrates why your idea is a good idea and how it can be implemented.

- Provides the benefits for the Government and how this would create awareness of living with dementia.

- Demonstrates your ability to creatively come up with a new and innovative idea.

# E-TRAY - TEST 2

# PART 1 OF THE E-TRAY EXERCISE

# BACKGROUND INFORMATION

The Department of Education provides many responsibilities in terms of educational opportunities. As stated on the Government website for the Department of Education, they hope "to achieve a highly educated society in which opportunity is equal for children and young people, no matter what their background or family circumstances".

# DEPARTMENT OF EDUCATION PRIORITIES

The Government want to ensure that opportunities and policies are created in order to maintain a sufficient education system. Top priorities for the Department of Education include:

- Self-improved school-led system.
- Remove unnecessary regulation and bureaucracy.
- Develop an effective workforce.
- Allocate funding fairly.
- Increase expectations of academia, school curriculums and assessments.

# YOUR JOB

You have recently joined the Department of Education as a Supervisor. There have been some issues left unattended and need to be addressed as soon as possible. You have previously completed a number of tasks concerning educational purposes.

The Managing Director has requested that you take charge of all matters for the next three weeks while he is away. The Managing Director believes that you can show strong performances in the role and will be able to manage the duties required. You are to deal with all issues whilst the Managing Director is away, and must only contact him with important or severe issues.

Business plans are ongoing regarding education. You need to maintain financial assurances, allocations of funding, assessing young people and opportunities and maintaining schooling systems.

## TEAM MEMBERS

**Peter Adams** – Managing Director. He deals with all the clarifications and makes the final decisions. Any resignations should be forwarded to him, so he can deal with them directly. He is in charge of making sure that new policies are signed and dated and checked before being implemented.

**Alecia Haynes** – Alecia is the secretary of the department. Any sickness or lateness should be reported to her as soon as possible. She deals with all the filing of documentation, including new and proposed policies and ideas. She looks after the filing system and makes sure everything is filed in the correct place. She also deals with telephone and email enquiries and points customers/people in the right direction.

**James Phillips** – supervisor. He supervises the whole education department. Any issues or questions should be forwarded to him before going to the Managing Director. He oversees his team and ensures that they are continuously on track, coming up with new ideas and enforcing them. Supervisors need to be well organised, confident, have an eye for detail and are able to show good communication, good teamwork and leadership skills.

## PLANNED EXPENDITURE 2014/2015

The Government proposed expenditures for the Department of Education are as follows:

| Area | £million |
| --- | --- |
| Pre – 16 | 49,172 |
| 16 to 19 | 7,675 |
| Administration | 75 |
| TOTAL | 56,922 |

# PROCESS OF IDEAS BEING IMPLEMENTED

If the Government decide to implement one of your ideas, there are a few simple instructions that need to be followed:

- If your idea has been accepted, you need to inform the rest of your team. The managing director, secretary and supervisors all need to be informed.
- You need to express what idea has been accepted and decide a formal action plan.
- As a team, come up with a list of ideas of how you are going to implement your idea and how it would be put it into action.
- Create an action plan of how you are going to proceed and send it to management to confirm.
- If management confirms, begin action on implementing new idea.
- Completed ideas and action plans need to be addressed and determined within one week, and active production should commence straight after.

# PART 2 OF THE E-TRAY EXERCISE - TEST 2

## Email 1

**Send**   Save   Discard

To:   yourname@gmail.com

Cc/Bcc:

Subject:   **Resignation Letter**

B   *I*   U   Normal     Normal   A ▾   ✎ ▾   **Link**   ≣ ≔ ⇥ ⇤ ▤ ▤ ▤ x₂ x² ᴬᴮᶜ 𝐓

-----,

It is with regret that I must hand in my letter of resignation. I know I have recently returned to work after the birth of my daughter, but I feel that my duties now rely at home.

I have greatly appreciated everything this company has offered me and I can safely say that I am going to miss working here.

Just to let you know, that I am still owed three weeks of my maternity pay. I am hoping that my last day could be no later than the 10th December

Thank you,
Mia Rowe

## Responses:

| | Most Effective | Least Effective |
|---|---|---|
| Forward the email on to Peter Adams and let him deal with the email. | | |
| Email back saying you have received her email and filed it. You have dealt with her resignation and will let Peter know on his return. | | |
| Do not reply to the email. The email does not require a response. | | |
| Forward on the email to your supervisor. You have not long been working at the department and therefore do not know the correct proceedings to file her resignation letter. | | |

## Email 2

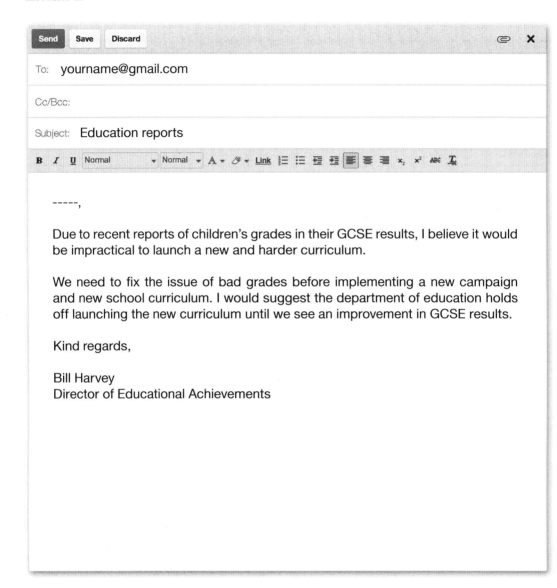

Send   Save   Discard

To:   yourname@gmail.com

Cc/Bcc:

Subject:   Education reports

B  *I*  U  Normal    ▾ Normal  ▾  A ▾  ✐ ▾  Link  ≣ ≔ ⬕ ⬔ ≣ ≣ ≣ x₂ x² ABC ✐

-----,

Due to recent reports of children's grades in their GCSE results, I believe it would be impractical to launch a new and harder curriculum.

We need to fix the issue of bad grades before implementing a new campaign and new school curriculum. I would suggest the department of education holds off launching the new curriculum until we see an improvement in GCSE results.

Kind regards,

Bill Harvey
Director of Educational Achievements

## Responses:

| | Most Effective | Least Effective |
|---|---|---|
| Go ahead and implement the new school curriculum. | | |
| Do a press conference stating the issues of education and how this needs to be improved and what the Government are thinking of doing. | | |
| Hold a meeting with everyone involved with implementing the new curriculum and decide how to move forward. | | |
| Email back thanking them for the email. | | |

## Email 3

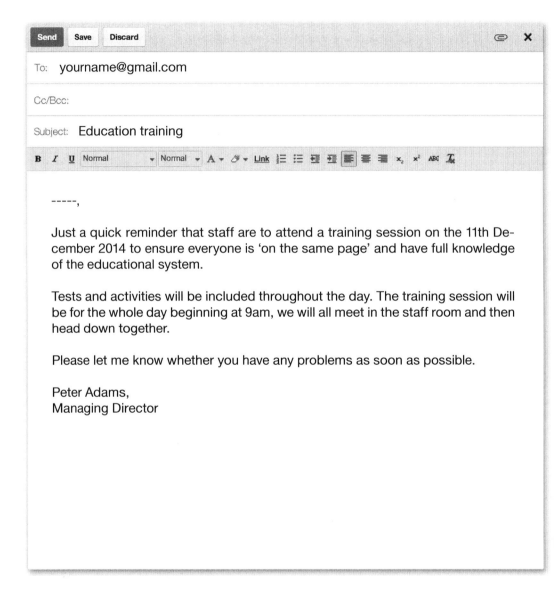

To: yourname@gmail.com

Cc/Bcc:

Subject: Education training

-----,

Just a quick reminder that staff are to attend a training session on the 11th December 2014 to ensure everyone is 'on the same page' and have full knowledge of the educational system.

Tests and activities will be included throughout the day. The training session will be for the whole day beginning at 9am, we will all meet in the staff room and then head down together.

Please let me know whether you have any problems as soon as possible.

Peter Adams,
Managing Director

## Responses:

| | Most Effective | Least Effective |
|---|---|---|
| Reply to Peter telling him you have received his email and you are able to attend the training session. | | |
| Email Alecia saying that you have an important meeting to attend that day, which conflicts with the training session. | | |
| Do not reply. | | |
| Reply to Peter and claim that you are unsure why you will be tested on the day. | | |

## Email 4

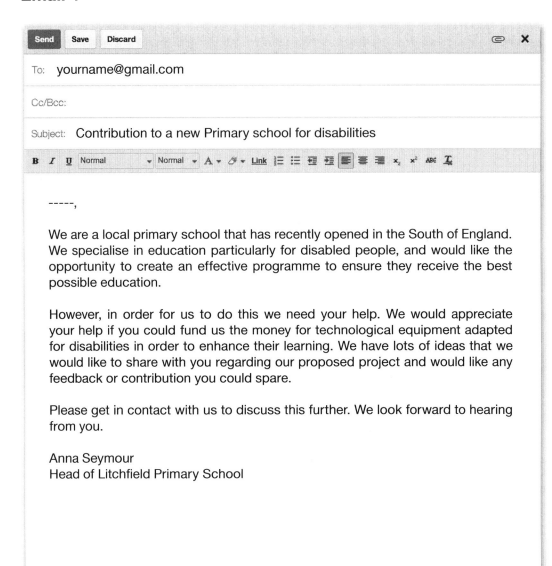

| Send | Save | Discard | | ⊜ ✕ |

To:    yourname@gmail.com

Cc/Bcc:

Subject:    Contribution to a new Primary school for disabilities

**B** *I* <u>U</u> Normal    ▾ Normal ▾ A ▾ ✐ ▾ Link ⠿ ⠿ ⇥ ⇤ | ▤ ▤ ▤ x₂ x² ABC 🅧

-----,

We are a local primary school that has recently opened in the South of England. We specialise in education particularly for disabled people, and would like the opportunity to create an effective programme to ensure they receive the best possible education.

However, in order for us to do this we need your help. We would appreciate your help if you could fund us the money for technological equipment adapted for disabilities in order to enhance their learning. We have lots of ideas that we would like to share with you regarding our proposed project and would like any feedback or contribution you could spare.

Please get in contact with us to discuss this further. We look forward to hearing from you.

Anna Seymour
Head of Litchfield Primary School

## Responses:

|  | Most Effective | Least Effective |
| --- | --- | --- |
| Reply back to the email accepting you are willing to contribute to such a well thought out programme. |  |  |
| Kindly reject this offer and wish them all the best for the future. |  |  |
| Forward the email to the Managing Director. |  |  |
| Ignore the email and do not tell anyone about it. |  |  |

## Email 5

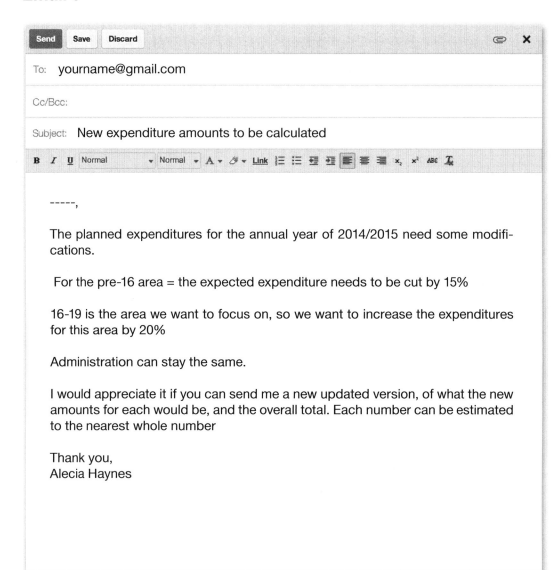

Send   Save   Discard

To:   yourname@gmail.com

Cc/Bcc:

Subject:   New expenditure amounts to be calculated

B   *I*   U   Normal    Normal   A ▾   ⟊ ▾   Link ⠿ ⠿ ⠿ ⠿ ⠿ ⠿ ⠿ x₂ x² ᴬᴮᶜ ⊥

-----,

The planned expenditures for the annual year of 2014/2015 need some modifi-
cations.

For the pre-16 area = the expected expenditure needs to be cut by 15%

16-19 is the area we want to focus on, so we want to increase the expenditures
for this area by 20%

Administration can stay the same.

I would appreciate it if you can send me a new updated version, of what the new
amounts for each would be, and the overall total. Each number can be estimated
to the nearest whole number

Thank you,
Alecia Haynes

## Responses:

| | Most Effective | Least Effective |
| --- | --- | --- |
| I am sorry, but I do not have the data to work this out. | | |
| The new projected income for pre 16 = £41,796,          16-19 = £9,210 and for Admin = £75. So the total will be = £51,081 | | |
| The new projected income for pre 16 = £36,218,          16-19 = £19,210 and for Admin = £75. So the total will be = £55,503 | | |
| The new projected income for pre 16 = £15,219,          16-19 = £17,857 and for Admin = £78. So the total will be = £33,154 | | |

# PART 3 OF E-TRAY EXERCISE – TEST 2

## Written Exercise

You have just received notification that you have received funding to implement a new education campaign regarding education and disabilities. You want to tell the rest of you team about this good news and need to come up with a strategy to proceed to the next stage. Write a short memo in the style of an email as to how you will tell the rest of your team members.

DRAFTS / NOTES

**Response:**

TO: --------

From: ------------

Date:

Subject:

# ANSWERS TO E-TRAY EXERCISE – TEST 2

## Email 1

Email back saying you have received her email and filed it. You have dealt with her resignation and will let Peter know on his return.

- *This would be the **MOST EFFECTIVE** response. You are in charge of all matters while Peter is away, however he will want to be notified on his return. Therefore this provides the most professional and correct way.*

Forward the email on to Peter Adams and let him deal with the email.

- *This is the **LEAST EFFECTIVE** response. Peter has asked that you deal with all matters while he is away. Emailing him with a resignation email does not comply with what he has asked and therefore demonstrates your lack of ability to follow orders.*

Do not reply to the email. The email does not require a response.

- *This is ineffective. You need to acknowledge an email like this so you can assure her that her resignation is being dealt with and has been filed.*

Forward on the email to your supervisor. You have not long been working at the department and therefore do not know the correct proceedings to file her resignation letter.

- *This is not an appropriate response. Your supervisor does not manage the resignation letters and he was not asked to handle these situations, therefore it would be inappropriate to make him handle this issue.*

## Email 2

Hold a meeting with anyone involved with implementing the new curriculum and decide how to move forward.

- *This would be the **MOST EFFECTIVE** response. It will allow everyone to know what's happening and come up with ideas on how to proceed.*

Go ahead and implement the new school curriculum.

• *This is the **LEAST EFFECTIVE** response. The issues of education need to be addressed before changes are implemented.*

Do a press conference stating the issues of education and how this needs to be improved and what the Government are thinking of doing.

• *This is unnecessary at this time. Doing a press conference when no decision has been made in regards to dealing with the issue is impractical.*

Email back thanking them for the email.

• *This is not a necessary response. It doesn't deal with the situation, and the email doesn't require a response.*

## Email 3

Reply to Peter telling him you have received his email and you are able to attend the training session.

• *This would be the **MOST EFFECTIVE** response because it assures the Managing Director that you are able to attend the training session and that you received his email.*

Email Alecia saying that you have an important meeting to attend that day, which conflicts with the training session.

• *This would be the **LEAST EFFECTIVE** response because you have emailed the wrong person in regards to the training session.*

Do not reply.

• *This is an ok response because the email only asks to get in contact if you have any problems, but it is polite to say that you received the email.*

Reply to Peter and claim that you are unsure why you will be tested on the day.

• *This is not an appropriate response. Everyone will be made to take the training session including all the tests to ensure everyone has the right knowledge and skills required. Therefore it would be inappropriate to question his judgement on the matter.*

## Email 4

Forward the email to the Managing Director.

- *This would be the MOST EFFECTIVE response because such decisions are too authoritative for your position and therefore the decision should be decided by management.*

Reply back to the email accepting you are willing to contribute to such a well thought out programme.

- *This is the LEAST EFFECTIVE response because you do not have the power or authority to sanction such funding for projects without the consent of management.*

Kindly reject this offer and wish them all the best for the future.

- *This response would not be your decision to make, so you shouldn't take it upon yourself to decline the email.*

Ignore the email and do not tell anyone about it.

- *Ignoring the email does not help anyone nor does it deal with the request. Thus this response would be immature and unprofessional.*

## Email 5

The new projected income for pre 16 = £41,796, 16-19 = £9,210 and for Admin = £75. So the total will be = £51,081

- *This would be the MOST EFFECTIVE response because it accurately calculates what has been asked.*

I am sorry, but I do not have the data to work this out.

- *This response would be the LEAST EFFECTIVE because you have been provided the information in the background information.*

The new projected income for pre 16 = £15,219, 16-19 = £17,857 and for Admin = £78. So the total will be = £33,154

- *This would not be appropriate because it gives the wrong calculations.*

The new projected income for pre 16 = £36,218, 16-19 = £19,210 and for Admin = £75. So the total will be = £55,503

- *This would not be an appropriate response because it gives the wrong calculations.*

## Written exercise

Your answer should be written in a professional and formal way. It doesn't have to be a long answer, it has to be straight to point and include all the relevant information. You need to be able to convey to your other team members that your idea has been accepted and what the way forward from here would be.

(Here is an example of what you could have written).

---

TO: ALL
From: -----------
Date: 14th November 2014
Subject:

I would like to inform you all that our **recent idea has been accepted** and we can **begin work creating a strategic plan** of how to implement it.

Management have decided to go with the **campaign for educational opportunities regarding people with disabilities.** Therefore I think it is wise that we all are 100% on board with this idea, and I expect **every effort from everyone** who is contributing to the project.

To move forward, **I think it is best if we arrange a day to meet,** all of us, so we can sit down and **come up with clear understanding and decision of how we are going to work on this project.** Please respond to this email and **give me a list of dates that you are free within the next week,** so we can start to **take immediate action** regarding this project.

Kind regards,

-----

---

- The email is professional and formal and grammatically correct.

- You have addressed everyone involved and described the idea that has been chosen and how you would like to proceed.

- You have stated that you need to meet everyone to ensure this project is put into place and have asked them all to give you dates that they are free within the next week in order to start immediately on the project.

# CHAPTER 7

# *GENERAL TIPS FOR PASSING E-TRAY EXERCISES*

# GENERAL TIPS FOR PASSING THE E-TRAY TESTS

## Responding to the emails exercise

1. All the emails that you respond to will be multiple choice. Therefore you need to remember that one or more of the responses may seem sufficient. You need to filter out the responses, analyse them in terms of accuracy, relevance, significance and effectivity.

*Helpful Tips*

2. Please be aware that the more emails you answer, the more emails that will arrive in your inbox. Be sure to continuously be on the lookout for new emails.

3. Remember to prioritise! Prioritise each email in regards to how important it is. An email that requires urgent attention, would be on your list of high priorities and therefore you should consider answering that email as quickly as possible.

4. **REMEMBER: Make sure you check emails for any attachments.**

5. Not all the information you will be presented with will be relevant to the emails you are answering. This is why it is important that you don't spend ages writing everything out word-for-word. Make clear and concise bullet points that you think may come in handy.

6. Attention to detail is crucial. Make sure you read the information thoroughly and ensure you have not misinterpreted the situation. Make sure your response has no silly errors.

## The written exercise

1. Your response should be well structured, logical, informative and analytical. Simply making points will not prove an adequate response. You need to probe deeper into your points and state why they're important, what's good and bad about them and why this would be beneficial.

2. It is important that in your response, you know who you are responding to. Addressing certain people may require a different type of response. For example, emailing back a colleague or a friend, your response may be more candid and friendly, whereas if you're emailing someone from a third party, your response should be professional and formal.

3. Understand that there may be more than one option or response that can be deemed adequate. Your task is to filter out the strengths and weaknesses and respond in the way you see necessary.

4. Ensure you have enough evidence, data and explanations to validate your response and state why it is the best way forward. You cannot base your argument on basic points, you cannot rely on assumptions. Your argument needs to be informative, analytical and important.

5. Make sure your argument concludes! There is no point writing a response and having no clear conclusion at the end. Be sure to thoroughly state what it is you are trying to say!

**Note:** although we are unable to provide you with an exact demonstration of what to expect in the E-Tray exercise, this practice test will give you some indication of the types of information, documents, attachments and other important data you may be presented with in the real E-Tray exercise!

# CHAPTER 8

## *ASSESSMENT CENTRE*

Your E-Tray test will have been assessed and shortlisted candidates who demonstrated great levels of competencies, skills and knowledge will be invited to attend a one day assessment. This is held at the Fast Stream Assessment Centre (FSAC) in London, where you will complete the final stages of the Civil Service assessment.

Assessment centres are used in selection processes to highlight and produce accurate results in determining strong candidates. Fast Stream standards are extremely high (as you would have learned from the tests you have previously completed), therefore you need to be able to show your personal qualities and the skills required to be a successful fast stream candidate.

## Fast Stream Assessment Centre (FSAC) in London

- You will have received an email, emailed to your Fast Stream inbox informing you of the time and date of the assessment.

- Allow time to travel to the assessment centre. Remember, London is busy and busy means traffic! So don't get caught up or you may not be able to participate in the assessment.

- Remember to bring your identification documents with you on the day of your assessment. (This may include your passport, national insurance number, birth certificate etc).

## What to expect...

- Upon arrival, your personal identification will be checked.

- You will then have to make your way into the centre whereby a member of Operations will complete your registration.

- This is the time where you can ask questions or concerns you may have about the day.

- You will receive a timetable for the day, and how your activities will be structured. Note that other people may have activities at different times to you, but you all do the same activities, just in different orders.

- "Try to relax, sleep well the night before. Remember you will not do as well on all the activities so try hard to compartmentalise them and do not let a perceived bad performance in one, affect you in the next – let it go". (Maya Desai, Fast Streamer candidate)

- The activities are designed to test your core skills and competencies in relation to Fast Stream roles.

- You will be given the opportunity to experience and sample typical activities that you would expect in the life of a Fast Streamer.

- These exercises will include a written assignment, group exercises, presentations and an interview.

Competencies is an important word in terms of the Civil Service. In order to prepare for the assessment centre, you should make a list of all the competencies that are required as a civil servant. Do your research beforehand. What are they going to be looking for? What will make you stand out from other candidates?

Below is a list of key competencies that will be evaluated on your one day assessment course. You should be able to come up with examples of each competency and demonstrate how you have portrayed yourself using that category. **You may find it useful to fill in the table below with recollections and examples of when you have demonstrated that skill.**

| | |
|---|---|
| **Seeing the 'bigger' picture** | |
| **Clarity of vision and ideas** | |

| | |
|---|---|
| **Changing and improving** | |
| **Leadership** | |
| **Making effective and important decisions** | |
| **Managing** | |
| **Delivering value for money** | |
| **Commercial outcomes** | |
| **Performance – ability to show integrity and diligence** | |
| **Collaborating with others** | |

The section below provides detailed information on each of the activities that you will participate in on the day of your assessment. It will provide you with information and examples to demonstrate possible scenarios you may be faced with.

# THE WRITTEN EXERCISE

- The written exercise will be conducted on a customised computer which will last approximately 1 hour and 45 minutes.

- During this time, you will need to complete two tasks.

- The first task will include a file of papers which will provide data and information about potential Government projects which can be used to resolve a problem. Your task is to analyse the papers and recommend which proposed project should be used. **REMEMBER: there is no wrong or right answer. You can pick either option as long as you conduct a clear and convincing argument as to why you chose it.** You need to structure your answer as a formal argument. Your argument should include detailed explanations, analysis, evidence and significance.

- The time limit may seem like a long time, but you will not have enough time to write a thorough draft, therefore it is advised that you work quickly and effectively through your answer.

- The second task follows on from the first. The papers that you have just read and the proposed solutions that were described should be taken into consideration to form your own additional ways of achieving a solution. Your option should implement the Government strategies and pay particular attention to the overall implications, significance and objectives which would result from your idea being implemented. This task is used to assess your performance based on making effective decisions, communication, seeing the bigger picture and other important competencies.

- Key competencies that are being assessed in your written test are **decision making skills, communication, planning, clear vision, seeing the 'bigger picture'** and **delivering an effective outcome.**

## Planning your written exercise...

- Although you are not told what subject areas you will be given to compare and contrast in order to write your answer, you can practice your writing style.

- An important part of the written exercise is to demonstrate an effective, clear and concise argument which highlights the relevance, importance and benefits of why you decided on the choice you made.

- Practice by reading articles on the same subject, and form your own conclusion. Read these articles and decide which article makes the argument better and why.

- Your writing style will also need to depend on the type of role you are applying for in the Civil Service. If you are applying for a business-orientated role, your writing style needs to be professional and 'business-like'. Adapting your writing style to your preferred job position clearly illustrates that you have taken the time to think about the selection process and how much it means to you.

- Practising written analysis methods such as the SWOT and PEST analysis will allow your writing to cover the main points. The SWOT analysis (strengths, weaknesses, opportunities and threats) will create an all-round argument and ensure you have covered most aspects of your choices. The PEST analysis (political, economic, social and technology) will filter your answer more specifically if writing an answer fitting one or more of these examples.

## Writing your response...

- You will be given a brief on the exercise along with background information regarding the scenario.

- Use your time wisely, and filter out the information provided based on the argument you want to make. There is no point reading through everything which may not be relevant to your final decision.

- Take care of your writing style. Punctuation, spelling, grammar, paragraphs etc. are all vital in demonstrating a successful written exercise.

- Make valid points and back them up with examples and evidence.

- Be convincing! You want to remain objective but still demonstrate an authoritative response.

## EXAMPLE – Written exercise scenario

**Summary** – in recent years, the UK has seen crime rate increase in certain neighbourhoods, particularly around London. Many of these crimes are youth related. Therefore the Government is trying to implement new incentives to tackle the number of youths participating in criminal activity. Your Minister has asked for advice on the best allocation of how to proceed. He has advised that the starting-up fund for this incentive can reach no higher than £5 million.

On the next page there are two options which you need to analyse and decide how to proceed:

| Option 1: Youth support schemes | Option 2: Scholarships |
|---|---|
| The £5 million will be invested in implementing support strategies for youth in neighbourhoods across the UK. The incentive will offer a way for the youth to remove themselves from criminal activity and start a fresh. | The £5 million will be used to create working schemes and scholarships for young people. The scheme will need 5% more than the total asking price. |
| This incentive will include youth centres and homes whereby young people can go to receive advice and support. It gives them a place to go which keeps them off the street. These centres will provide a friendly atmosphere and play host to a small-scale entertainment centre. | The working schemes will be put in place to ensure young people are fully prepared, fully equipped and ready to work. |
| Homes will be offered for young people who are in troubling circumstances and need another place to go. Young people do not want to feel like they are unwelcome somewhere, and often do not want to ask for help. These homes however provide a place for them to stay and get back on their feet. | These schemes will provide education for people who struggled in school or want to achieve more qualifications. This scheme provides work placements, experience and real-life activities that they can engage with and help them understand the life of a worker. |
| It does have some concerns. Setting up this incentive would take several years, and by that point, youth employment and crime rates may have decreased. Although it is estimated a 3% loss in profits in the first 2 years, the scheme is said to have long-lasting effects that will ensure an effective and sufficient society. | Scholarships will be designed to inspire young people to achieve something more. These scholarships will be implemented abroad, as well as in the UK, in hope to inspire young people to apply and gain experience in any job, anywhere. |
| | This incentive will require help from international support. Therefore money will be taken internationally in aid to support the scheme. The Government need to be fully aware of the profits and the effect it will have on society. The scheme is estimated to make a 5% decrease in the amount of youth crime in the first 3 years of being launched. |

This is a basic example of the type of comparison you could expect in your written exercise. So, your task is to work out which option the Government should implement. You are not provided with a great deal of information, but it does give you an insight into the benefits of each option and how the incentive aims to be achieved.

We have provided you with space to make some notes on how you would respond. Remember, there is no right or wrong answer, as long as you use the information to back up your information. We recommend you use the advice provided earlier on in this chapter to practice these types of questions.

NOTES:

# THE GROUP EXERCISE OR 'ROLE PLAY'

- The Group Exercise is designed to test the candidate's ability to make effective decisions, work alongside other team members, show leadership and communicate effectively.

- Sometimes this exercise may be described as a 'role play' and to some extent it is. You are put in a fictitious scenario, therefore you need to pretend to have the job given to you in the brief. You need to take the role seriously and fully comprehend what is being asked.

- Your group will consist of 5 or 6 people, and you will be given a fictitious scenario which you will need to evaluate and form a proposal.

- You will usually be given a number of options, and it is your group's task to recommend an option and provide support and evidence to back up your reasoning for this conclusion.

- You will be given approximately 50 minutes to complete this task.

- At the beginning of the exercise, you will be provided with background information about the brief, the scenario and the main issues which need to be addressed.

- All group members will receive the same core material, however each individual will be given an assigned, individual brief. It is your task to come up with the best outcome for the position which you are representing.

- Key competencies that will be evaluated in this task include **making effective decisions, collaborating with others, leadership, communicating** and **delivering value for money.**

## Preparation time...

- You will be given approximately 30 minutes to prepare for this exercise on your own. During this time, it is advised that you make the most out of the preparation time.

- During this preparation time, list all of the points that you think are relevant to the discussion. Somebody else in your group may mention one of your points, so you should feel comfortable enough to engage in the discussion and develop the point further.

- Listen to others. They may say something that you have not thought of or they may have looked at something from a different view point to you.

- You may feel that the time limit for the preparation is not enough. If you do not have enough time to finish reading all the material and background information in the brief, decide what you want to say and why. Then use the information from the brief to pinpoint your argument.

## Discussion time...

- Ensure everyone in your group makes a contribution to the discussion. It is a group exercise and therefore you will get marked collaborating with other people.

- Try to avoid taking notes during the discussion time. You want to make sure that you are paying attention to what is being said and that you show interest into what other people have to say.

- If you can, try to voice your opinions in the discussion as early as you can. You want to show your enthusiasm and it is likely that being one of the first people to speak, will leave an impression on the assessors.

- Try to avoid being shy and timid. You do not want to have a laid back approach. Assert your views and opinions and make sure you demonstrate that you have something to say, and what you say is worthwhile listening to.

- Be prepared to alter your opinions and thoughts after hearing other people's views. This shows the assessors that you are willing to support somebody else's claims.

- Do not take criticism personally. Someone may not agree with what you have to say, but that is no reason to get upset or disheartened. Stand your ground and try to win them over. If unsuccessful, listen to what they have to say and respond to their views showing you disagree and the reasons why.

- Key competencies to be analysed in the group exercise / role play are **developing ideas, teamwork, planning, communication and performance.**

## EXAMPLE - Group exercise scenario

**Scenario** – tackling youth unemployment in contemporary society

**Brief** – due to the recent recession over the last 10 years, society has been majorly struck down by unemployment. This resulted in a lot of people being 'let go', and finding it hard to get a job. Fundamentally, this effected youth the most. Young people struggled to find work, particularly after leaving full time education with little or no qualifications.

You are a member of a Governmental group (made up of 5 people) whose aim is to come up with a solution in order to help fix the issue of youth unemployment.

**Positions** – There are 5 members in your team; there are five options from five different departments:

1. Youth volunteers
2. National internships
3. New incentives of apprenticeships
4. Employer incentives
5. Employment training

**Pointers** – You need to come up with the best option for tackling youth unemployment in contemporary society. Your argument needs to explain why you chose it, the benefits of it, why it's the best option as opposed to others, possible issues and resolutions etc.

- The group exercise does not have a wrong or right answer.

- The brief will include important information regarding each option and therefore your argument should often refer back to this data and information.

- Remember, each individual in the group will be assigned a brief to match one of these options. It is their job to negotiate their position as being the right choice.

- Remember to listen to what other people have to say, and use their responses to reflect your own reasoning and analysis.

# THE PRESENTATION

- The presentation is another important assessment that you can expect to take at the assessment centre.

- You will be notified about everything you will be expected to participate in prior to the assessment day, so it gives you plenty of time to practice and prepare for the presentation.

- You will not know the subject of your presentation until a short time before you actually have to make it. Therefore, you need to make sure you are well-versed in a number of potential scenarios that could be used during the presentation.

- These scenarios could range from anything concerning the Government. For example, health and safety, the environment, legislation, new policies and regulations, equality etc.

- Some of these scenarios may overlap and you will be able to use your research to make important points.

## Before the day of your presentation...

- Because you are not given the subject of your presentation until the day, it will be hard to structure what you are going to say.

- However, you can research into possible subject areas (as mentioned in the previous paragraph) as to how you may go about tackling a presentation on that area.

- Bullet point important information for each subject area which you can reference in the presentation.

- Although you cannot fully structure your presentation, you can come up with a basic structure to take some of the pressure off. Start by making an introduction that reflects Governmental issues and highlight what you want to convey throughout the presentation. In your conclusion, you want to make sure you have rounded up all your key points and formed a solid and reasonable conclusion.

## Preparing for your presentation...

- A short while before you are asked to give your presentation, you will receive a brief and the topic of your presentation.

- From here you can tailor all your research to fit the criteria of the presentation.

- The briefing pack will include your subject, time limit and some information surrounding your topic.

- Make sure you write down all what you want to say. Many candidates find the time limit a strain and hard to stick to, therefore you want to make sure all your important points are put across as early as possible.

## Your presentation...

- Talk about both the advantages and disadvantages of your argument, how is it beneficial, what are the downfalls, are there other alternatives to consider. If you don't answer these questions yourself, you are more likely to be asked them by the assessors in the follow up questions, so try to show you have already thought about these issues in your presentation.

- Your success rate of your presentation can be determined by your efforts and work you put in during the preparation time. Therefore, it is fundamental that you make the best of that time to ensure your best performance.

- The assessors do not expect a well-versed and polished performance in your presentation. What they do expect is that you can take a brief and show your understanding and ideas about a subject area despite having little knowledge about it.

- As in any presentation, you will want to make sure that you keep good eye contact, speak slowly and clearly and demonstrate confidence in what you are saying.

- A timely presentation is important. If you find yourself running out of time, make sure you have said all the important information you wanted to get across.

- Be ready to answer any follow up questions. The assessors may have picked up on something you said and want to talk about it in more detail. Be prepared and make sure you provide a valid response.

- The assessors in follow up questions usually ask as many questions as possible until it looks like you have nothing else to say. This isn't to undermine your performance, nor is it to make you look like a weak candidate, they do this to highlight your ability to put forward your views when put on the spot.

# THE INTERVIEW

- The one-to-one interview will last approximately 45 minutes.

- A Civil Service interview usually consists of two or three people asking you a set of structured questions, questions that would be asked to all candidates. This is called a 'structured' interview whereby everyone receives the same questions, however, they may not receive the same follow-up questions.

- The importance of the interview is to evaluate your performance in relation to the competencies that have previously been mentioned.

- You need to work out what the question is asking you, what competency it relates to and provide a convincing answer to show evidence and examples.

- Try not to use the same examples for more than one competency. You need to show the ability that you have experienced a range of competencies at different times.

## Before the Interview...

- You may want to come up with a list of examples and evidence to use in your interview. This will not only allow you to show a range of skills and competencies, but it will also take off the pressure you will be feeling to think on your feet!

- Drawing from personal experiences such as school, university and life will demonstrate high levels of critical-thinking.

- Despite filling in an application form prior to the assessment day, your assessors will not have seen any of the information you have supplied. Therefore you should try your best to make a good first impression!

## During the Interview...

- The assessors will explore each competency which you must respond with a clear example of having used that competency in the past.

- You can ask for the information that you disclose in the interview to remain confidential, and you can ask the assessors not to talk about anything that may be particularly sensitive to you.

- Be honest! The assessors will be able to tell if you are making something up, or if you come across as unprepared. Do your research! Make sure you are fully prepared for the interview.

- The interview stage isn't a trick or a trap, it's a way of assessing your qualities, experiences and personality to ensure you are a suitable candidate to join the Civil Service.

## How to prepare for the Interview...

- A guide will be sent to you before the assessment centre day.

- It is imperative that you carefully read through the guide and understand what is expected of you on the day of your assessment.

- The guide will inform you what the assessors are looking for and what they are expecting in terms of your skills and competencies.

- After reading through the guide, it would be wise to write down key points, thoughts and any experience and skills that come to mind. You need to be able to express these skills through experiences. So try and come up with as many experiences as possible. The more experiences you come up with, the more prepared you will feel.

- It is likely that in the interview you will be asked about learning from past mistakes and times when you have stepped out of your comfort zone. These are not to trick you! They are a way of exploring how well you can adapt to a situation and provide a solution to a problem. What did you learn from this? What would you do differently?

- Filling in the table presented at the beginning of the chapter, regarding competencies, is a great way to get you started! You can keep adding to the list which will make you feel more relaxed and confident when it comes to your interview.

## Potential interview questions...

- Name a time when you followed an action plan.

- Describe a time when you worked as part of a team.

- Why do you want to work as a member of the Civil Service?

- When have you demonstrated leadership skills?

- Name a time when you have had to influence other people.

- Have you ever achieved a set of aims and objectives within a limited timescale?

- Have you ever had to prioritise your workload? How did you do this?

- Can you give an example when you have had to change your viewpoint or revised your work?

- Can you give an example where you have showed integrity and diligence?

- What are your key qualities?

- What are your weaknesses? How would you overcome these?

- Can you demonstrate a time when you took control of a situation and led it to success?

- Describe a time when you have made an important decision.

- Describe a situation where you have performed under pressure.

- What are your opinions on current affairs (assessors may name an example)

- Name a time where you have dealt with conflict with another person. How did you respond to this?

- How do you know what sources of information are credible?

- What goals have you set for yourself in regards to your possible role as a Fast Streamer?

- How did you prepare and plan for this interview?

## Interview technique...

The Civil Service interview is just like any other interview. Standard techniques still apply, and although they may seem quite obvious to you, many fail to comply with them on the day of their interview.

Here is a list of the key information you will need to know to make sure your interview technique is great and you are fully prepared to take on that all important interview.

1. **Be prepared!** You will be told about your interview when you receive your assessment guide prior to the assessment day. That means there is no reason for you not to be fully prepared and confident with your performance. You are having this interview for a reason – to join the Civil Service! Therefore it is imperative that you put 100% into the planning and execution of your assessment. With great effort comes great results! Don't fail at the last hurdle!

2. **Do your research!** This is similar to the stage above. Prepare for the interview! Do this by planning ahead, write down notes and pointers, come up with a list of what they may ask you and come up with your responses beforehand. Doing your research will not only make you perform better on the day of your interview, but it will allow you to feel that little bit more confident and relaxed.

3. **Tailor your skills and experience!** You are applying for a Fast Streamer job in the Civil Service. Therefore you need to be able to apply previous experience, skills and knowledge to the job you are applying for. If you

are asked 'what experience do you have?' you want to make sure you tailor your answer to fit the requirements for the role. If you don't have exact experience in that particular area, you can use an example and demonstrate how it could be applied to that job role. It's all about adapting your answers to ensure a successful response.

4. **Ask questions!** Just because you are the one being interviewed, this does not mean you cannot ask questions yourself. Asking questions demonstrates your enthusiasm and ability to get involved. This will show your assessors your keen interest for the job! Try to remain self-reflective and considerate in both your answers and questions. You want to be able to demonstrate your strengths and weaknesses by highlighting your assets and indicate why you would be the ideal person for the role.

5. **Good technique!** This interview will be similar to all the previous interviews you've had before. So, remember all the small details! Turn up to your assessment smartly dressed and well presented. Have a warm smile on your face and show a confident attitude. Remember, your body posture and gestures are very important too. For example, standing up straight, initiating the handshake, smiling etc. These are all finer details that really do make a difference. You want to make a good and lasting impression on your assessors. You do not want to be let down by your lack of interviewing technique!

6. **Be yourself!** This may seem like an obvious statement, but a lot of candidates go into an interview pretending to be someone that they are not. The best thing to do for any interview is to be yourself. Showing that you fully comprehend who you are is an admirable quality and the assessors will value this. You want to get the job for who you are; you shouldn't have to change that!

7. **Be confident, be yourself and be prepared!**

8. Key competencies that will be analysed at this stage are **planning** and **organising, taking responsibility, management,** and **drive for results.**

# FINAL SELECTION BOARD

After the Fast Stream Assessment Centre stage, you will receive your report based on your performance. You will receive this report whether you are successful or not. This report will contain feedback throughout your assessment and how well you did at each exercise. You can download your report from the Fast Stream website.

After the Fast Stream Assessment Centre, some schemes/options require you to attend a Final Selection Board. This will assess further skills and competencies. The schemes that will be asked to attend the Final Selection Board are:

- Diplomatic Service

- Houses of Parliament

- Science and Engineering

- Digital and Technology

- Government Communications Service


Schemes that do not require you to attend a Final Selection Board:

- European Fast Stream – unless you are considering a position in the Foreign and Commonwealth Office (FCO).

- Analytical Fast Stream

- Central Departments / Northern Ireland / HR / Commercial and Finance


You will receive more information tailored to your option/scheme before you attend the Final Selection Board.

# CHAPTER 9

# *GENERAL TIPS FOR PASSING ASSESSMENT CENTRE*

# HELPFUL TIPS FOR THE ASSESSMENT CENTRE

- Try to remember the key competencies that you are going to be assessed on during your day at the assessment centre.

- Refer to these competencies throughout the day. Remember, your mark will be based on how well you perform and your ability to reflect these competencies through a variety of scenarios and examples.

*Helpful Tips*

- Prior to attending the assessment centre, you will receive your assessment centre guide. Be sure to read through the guide carefully. It may help to read the guide more than once to ensure that you are fully prepared and know exactly what to expect on the day.

- There is a lot of information online regarding the Civil Service. Be sure to do your research and understand what is expected in the job role, particularly for Fast Streamers. You want to show that you know what you are talking about and know exactly why you want to join the Civil Service.

- This may sound obvious, but make sure you get a good night's sleep the night before. Having a good night's sleep will ensure that you perform at your full potential.

- Make sure you give yourself plenty of time to get to the assessment centre. The assessment centre is in London, so you need to expect traffic and delays!

- Remember, other candidates in your group are not your enemy. You do not have to compete with them. Everyone in the group is being assessed in the same way.

- Be yourself. The Civil Service is open to a range of different personalities, so you don't have to act the same as everyone else. It is likely that if you do something that stands out to the assessors, you are going to be remembered.

- For every activity you participate in, make sure you read the instructions and briefs set out extremely carefully. You do not want to miss any information that may be valuable to you. Eye for small details is a crucial step to success.

- Remember, this is the Fast Stream route. Therefore every activity assesses your 'speed' in order to reflect the demands of a Fast Stream job.

Good luck with your Civil Service Fast Stream Tests. We wish you the best of luck with all your future endeavours!

*The how2become team*

The How2become team

how2become

**Get more books, manuals, online tests and training courses at:**

**www.How2Become.com**